BEDFORD TO BERLIN
and beyond

ROBERT COATES

BEDFORD
TO BERLIN
and beyond

FITZJAMES PRESS

THE FITZJAMES PRESS
an imprint of
MOTOR RACING PUBLICATIONS LTD
Unit 6, The Pilton Estate, 46 Pitlake, Croydon, CR0 3RY, England

First published 1994

British Library Cataloguing in Publication Data
Coates, Robert
  Bedford to Berlin and Beyond:QL - The
  Forces' Favourite 4 x 4
  I. Title
  623.747

  ISBN 0-948358-05-X

Typeset by Express Typesetting Ltd, Croydon, Surrey

Printed and bound in Great Britain by
Hartnolls Ltd, Bodmin, Cornwall.

Contents

Foreword

This book tells the story of one of the most interesting load-carrying vehicles ever built. Pieced together from incomplete and disparate records, museum exhibits, books, anecdotes, old soldiers' and airmen's fond recollections – as well as a lifetime of fascination with the 'QL', the story covers this Bedford 3-tonner from evolution to peacetime activity, concentrating particularly on the many and vital roles it played during World War Two.

Despite numerous contradictory 'clues' present in the surviving material, this account gives as accurate a picture as I have been able to construct. Other records may still exist which could shed further light on the subject, and there will be people intimately involved with QLs who will be able to provide fact where I can only provide deduction and conjecture. I ask these experts to bear with me or, better still, to confirm the facts of the matter. For those who are less well-informed, this account will, I hope, provide them with useful and interesting information on the QL and, at least partially, explain my own obsession with the marque.

Part of the reason for this obsession may lie in the fact that the QL was the first vehicle in which I have any recollection of travelling. My father, to whose memory, together with that of my mother, I should like to dedicate this book, was an RASC driver during World War Two and I can recall, as a toddler, riding in the back (of a QLT) and being thoroughly spoiled by the Tommies who plied me with biscuits which appeared from 6lb tins stowed under the seats – all very exciting, but something about that day has stayed with me all my life and perhaps even shaped my career, which has ended up in transport consultancy!

Certainly, for many people, the sight and, perhaps particularly, the sound of the QL is very evocative. The fact that so many have survived into preservation is indicative of the high regard in which they are held. What it is that makes Bedford's QL so special will be seen in due course, but just to whet the appetite, consider that it went from concept, through design to prototype in just 22 weeks; that it spent a mere couple of months undergoing testing and was then put into production with barely any modifications; that over 52,000 were built during the war years and that a few are still earning a living over 50 years later, and you will have some idea that this was not just an ordinary piece of kit.

Many people have helped with the compilation of this book, and in particular I must thank David Fletcher, of the Tank Museum, who made access to the original WD Contracts possible as well as giving support and encouragement generally, and to Norman Holding, son of one of the QL's designers, who first set me on the track of serious research. There are others, too numerous to mention individually, who have provided anecdotes and photographs, and to all of them I am most grateful.

I can only hope that you will obtain as much pleasure from reading this account as I have had from researching and writing it.

March 1994   Robert Coates

The first QL, a QLD prototype, which was delivered to the War Department on February 1, 1940, for testing. Note how it differs from the eventual production version by its tyres, hubs and other subtleties. The 'PASS' plate was designed to be reversible, with regimental or unit markings on the other side. Within four weeks, a further two vehicles had been delivered and QL-1 returned to Luton for retention as the manufacturer's 'test bed'. Series production started in February 1941.

CHAPTER 1

Overlord

THE SIXTH OF JUNE, 1944. D-Day. The start of Operation Overlord and the Allied invasion of Normandy – the greatest invasion in the history of mankind. Never before had there been such concentrations of troops, armour, artillery and support vehicles combined to accomplish a single task.

Five beaches were selected for the invasion, three under British command and two under United States command. Under the command of the 2nd British Army were 1st British Corps, consisting of 3rd British Division which attacked Sword Beach, the most easterly point of the invasion, and 3rd Canadian Division which attacked Juno Beach. The most westerly of the British beaches was Gold Beach which was the job of 30 Corps, consisting of 50 (N) Division. To their west was the 1st US Army Group made up of 5 US Corps with 1 US Division and 29 US Division attacking Omaha Beach and, furthest west of all, 4 US Division making up 7 US Corps attacking Utah Beach.

The *fighting* story of D-Day, the Battle of Normandy and the subsequent events, battles and setbacks leading up to the German surrender at Luneburg Heath on Saturday May 5, 1945, does not need repeating here. Yet what of the vehicles and equipment, used in such unprecedented quantities to supply this mammoth undertaking? How, in a single day – June 6, 1944 – in the British sector alone and under such terrible conditions, was a total of 8,900 vehicles and 1,900 tons of stores, in addition to all the fighting troops, tanks and artillery, landed? How, with ultimately many hundreds of thousands of Allied troops deployed far from their bases, were they supplied with food, water, ammunition, petrol, oil, lubricants and other stores and equipment? How, too, was the advance through Europe, starting in France, spreading through Belgium and Holland and eventually right over to the Rhine and the Baltic, pressed home?

A QLD reversing into a Landing Craft–Assault, possibly as practice for the D-Day landings, although the absence of the Allies' star marking could indicate that it was practice for any of the seaborne landings which took place during the war.

Transport reinforcements arrive at the bridgeheads during the liberation of Europe in 1944. Masses of shipping reinforced the troops who were already on French soil with further men, vehicles, armour and equipment. The picture was taken looking down on vehicles leaving a Landing Ship-Tank – as distinct from a Landing Craft-Tank – as they make for the beaches.

Pioneers work on essential road drainage in the pouring rain while the Allied columns push on during August and September 1944. The censor has, again, been active on this photograph, eradicating the divisional markings on the QL.

The answer is that a vast fleet of lorries was used, day and night, initially direct from the beaches and, later, as they were recaptured, from the ports and ultimately, serving the recaptured railheads as the attack pressed deeper into occupied territory. Tens of thousands of British, American and Canadian trucks were to be seen, amongst which, in huge numbers, was the Bedford 4x4 3-tonner, the QL.

Yet the story of how the Allies prepared for the invasion starts long before June 1944. The general idea was conceived within days of Dunkirk, in the summer of 1940. Plans were laid in outline for a cross-channel thrust, without having selected in any detail exactly which areas and beaches would be involved. It was, though, clear from the onset that, with the large distances involved, the administrative and logistical back-up would be a major element. Production, at home and in the United States and Canada, was stepped up on all sorts of equipment as well as vehicles and special types which, as will be seen, were designed and accepted or rejected for specific duties connected with a predominantly seaborne invasion.

The final concentration of resources in readiness for Operation Overlord started in early 1944. Troops and vehicles could be seen all over the south-east of England and westwards along the south coast. There were even concentrations of dummy vehicles and tanks, mocked-up either from wood or inflatable, made of a similar material to the barrage balloons which were a common wartime sight. These were deployed so that enemy aerial reconnaissance would be misled into believing that the attack would be along a different route from that actually chosen.

So successful were these decoys that, even after the invasion had started, the German commanders, still believing that *Normandy* was the feint and that the real attack would come across the Pas de Calais, did not call up their badly-needed reserves to the Normandy area until it was too late for them to be effective.

As the great day approached, early echelons of troops and vehicles were called forward for embarkation and loading, the reserve echelons took their place, and so on down the line. It is difficult to comprehend the sheer scale of the operation, but the following table gives an idea of just how many personnel were moved through the despatch areas in the amazingly short space of a few days. These are the second and subsequent echelons so do not include those who were already embarked for the first wave.

The 51st Highland Division passing through Rouen in early September, 1944. The vehicle is a QLT, one of a batch of 1,500 vehicles, 500 of which were delivered in 1942 and the remainder in 1944. This is probably one of the earlier ones, having no cab-top hatch. War-survivors from this batch were converted to GS Offices during the Fifties.

Build-up of personnel for the landings

	D+1	D+2	D+3	D+4	D+5
Newhaven	4,750	495	660	-	-
Portsmouth	20,373	6,805	6,570	4,920	6,740
P'mth or Soton	24,987	-	-	-	-
Southampton	23,456	-	5,400	3,900	3,000
Felixstowe	10,600	-	-	-	-
Tilbury	11,900	23,500	1,920	2,520	2,520
London	18,960	-	4,800	6,000	6,000
Daily total	**115,026**	**30,800**	**18,350**	**17,340**	**18,560**

Thereafter followed a sustained intake of nearly 20,000 men per day.

In the event, despite the bad weather which adversely affected what could be achieved, most of the landing plans were actually exceeded. For example, the plan called for a cumulative total of 245,100 men, 32,429 vehicles and nearly 69,000 tons of stores and equipment – of which nearly half was ammunition – to have been landed by D+6, on June 12. At this stage the major part of the lift was still on pre-loaded lorries discharging from landing craft, although coasters

By September 4, 1944, Allied troops were in Brussels and were cheered and welcomed by the crowds which turned out to greet them. Two of Bedford's peace-time advertising slogans come to mind: "You see them everywhere" and "Suitable for 50% overload!"

were assisting the process, unloading at the Mulberry artificial harbours. However, even this Mulberry traffic ended up on the back of a lorry. The actual achievement against the plan was 326,000 men, 54,000 vehicles and 104,000 tons of stores. On top of this was a total of 2,104 tanks – and all in six days!

In the days and weeks that followed, men, vehicles and stores continued to pour ashore as one battle success after another was consolidated. Bad weather continued to affect operations and by late June, the memoirs of Field Marshal The Viscount Montgomery of Alamein tell us, "...some eight hundred craft of all types [had been] damaged or driven ashore... Except to a very limited extent...loading came to a standstill and it has been estimated that the overall unloading loss caused by the gale [19-22 June] was in the neighbourhood of 20,000 vehicles and 140,000 tons of stores."

Clearly, volumes such as those that were being moved caused enormous traffic congestion behind the beaches. By D+50, some 631,000 personnel, 153,000 vehicles and 689,000 tons of stores plus 68,000 tons of petrol, oil and lubricants had been brought ashore. 'Monty' records that "...at one check post 18,836 vehicles passed in one day, giving an hourly average of 785 vehicles, or one every four seconds throughout the twenty-four hours."

Fortunately, the detailed planning paid off, with, for the most part, targets being exceeded. What seems staggering is the vast number of vehicles involved, the largest proportion of which, especially in the earliest stages, were 4x4 3-tonners. These were engaged in every sphere during the landings, possibly none more so than the gargantuan task of simply clearing the beaches. Again, tables best serve to illustrate, not only the detail in which the plans had to be laid, but also the numbers of 4x4s involved. The following table, extracted from the personal notebook of the Colonel Quartermaster for Operation Overlord, a document which has only recently come to light, shows how the ubiquitous four-wheel-drive 3-tonner was phased-in for beach-group and sub-area tasks.

Phasing-in of 4x4 3-tonners
Beach-group and sub-areas clearance

	Gold	Juno	Sword	Mulberry
D	60	120	60	-
D+1	60	-	60	-
D+2	-	30	-	-
D+3	-	-	-	120
D+4	-	-	-	-
D+7	-	-	-	115
Totals	**120**	**150**	**120**	**235**
		Grand total 625		

The initial deployment of transport for beach clearance in the British sector is shown clearly in the next table. DUKWs, the GMC produced six-wheel-drive amphibious lorries with a 2½-ton payload, played a large role in bringing supplies ashore, especially in the very early stages when their ability to 'swim' was a major asset. At the same time 3-tonners and, to a lesser extent, the DUKWs, were being used for 'through' movements of troops and supplies as well as all the other myriad tasks which will be examined. The numbers shown in the table are those engaged solely in clearing the beaches and exclude any reserve vehicles, the total number of which amounted to the equivalent of a further 10 per cent.

British sector
Initial deployment of transport for beach clearance

	4x4 3-ton	DUKW
Sword:	39 Gen Tpt Coy (4 Pls)	101 Gen Tpt Coy (3 Pls)
		299 Gen Tpt Coy (3 Pls)
		633 Gen Tpt Coy (1 Pl) specially fitted for medical evacuation
Juno:	282 Gen Tpt Coy (4 Pls)	199 Gen Tpt Coy (3 Pls)
	551 Gen Tpt Coy (1 Pl)	297 Gen Tpt Coy (3 Pls)
		50 Gen Tpt Coy (3 Pls)
		633 Gen Tpt Coy (1 Pl as above)
Gold:	305 Gen Tpt Coy (4 Pls)	536 Gen Tpt Coy (3 Pls – may be Terrapins)
		705 Gen Tpt Coy (3 Pls)
		168 Gen Tpt Coy (3 Pls)
		633 Gen Tpt Coy (1 Pl as above)
Mulberry:	435 Gen Tpt Coy (4 Pls)	9 Gen Tpt Coy (3 Pls)*
	706 Gen Tpt Coy (4 Pls)	377 Gen Tpt Coy (3 Pls)*
		* may be Terrapins
Yapton:	714 Gen Tpt Coy (2 Pls)	none

Towards the end of November 1944, by which time the Allies had gained the upper hand, the advance continues along a canal bank as guns and troops of the 8th Corps KSLI Anti-Tank move on, over and past obstacles like fallen trees and broken down and abandoned enemy vehicles.

For every element of transport taking part in the landings, tasks were specified in minute detail and there were pages of typed notes and instructions, right down to individual platoons, stating precisely what had to be done, when and by whom. The following random extracts from the initial employment orders for transport columns

By January 1945, large numbers of POWs had been captured and these had to be transported back behind the lines where they could take no further part in the proceedings. Here they are at Bourg Leopold 'embussing' into a TCV which was used for transporting prisoners from one cage to another.

and companies of the RASC indicate the detail involved:

"The first portion of 318 Army Tps Comp Coy, consisting of one platoon of 4x4 3-tonners, will land on D+10 to assist the lift of RE stores to dumps and sites. The last portion, consisting of two platoons of 4x4 3-ton tippers, will land on D+15 for work with RE (Works) on road maintenance in the Army Area and forward."

"CRASC 20 Tpt Coln: one portion only will land on D+8. Its task will be the control of all specific, foreseen, transport details i.e. RAF and Royal Engineers' commitments." This was described as "...a difficult and fluctuating task requiring close liaison with the users" and it was stressed that the success of the operation largely depended on the service provided for airfield construction, and the subsequent RAF maintenance.

"The first portion (one platoon) of 551 GT Coy will land on D+2 with 1 Corps for beach clearance on sectors M/N. The remaining three platoons will land on D+5 to be available to assist beach clearance or for local transport. Finally, on D+8 the balance of the Company and the workshops will land."

Many other vehicle types, apart from 4x4 3-tonners, were, of course, involved in the landings and the subsequent operations up to the end of the war. Three tons was the standard payload rating for

Following good, clear weather over the Christmas period, bad weather set in during January 1945, causing some slowing of the advance. Here a driver wipes snow from his windscreen during a halt.

16

many of the services' vehicles, but there were many heavier examples – up to 10 tons payload – of so-called 'low mobility' vehicles, suitable only for on-road use. There were also lighter vehicles, notably of 15cwt payload, of which many thousands were employed. Not all 3-tonners were four-wheel drive – in fact most of them were simple 4x2s – and some of those which were four-wheel drive, were, in fact, six-wheelers – in other words, 6x4 – notably those of American manufacture.

Of the 4x4 3-tonners, some were 'normal control' – that is, with a bonnet – but, by far the most common in this category were the forward-control types. For the war period as a whole, production of 4x4 3-tonners amounted to about 111,000 vehicles; the QL represented nearly half of the total, from which it can be deduced that if a 4x4 was seen on D-Day, it was an even chance that it was a Bedford QL.

In Chapter 2, a more detailed examination will be made of some of the other makes and models but, almost certainly, the best known and loved of them all was the Bedford QL.

RAF crewmen moor an inflated barrage balloon for use as protection against German planes over a bridge which combat engineers of the 9th US Army, as part of 21st Army Group under Montgomery, are building across the Rhine. The eastern bank of this great river was reached on March 23, 1945, between Rees and Wesel.

CHAPTER 2

The beginning

The first Bedford QL was produced in February 1940, but that is almost the end of the story. The beginning was much earlier, although it is difficult to decide exactly when the story really starts.

Much had been learned about the technical aspects of military vehicle requirements during World War One. Perhaps not quite so thoroughly learned was the lesson that one should be in a state of constant readiness because, in September 1939, Britain was decidedly unprepared for a war with Germany. In his memoirs Churchill may well have used the title *The Gathering Storm* to describe the years leading up to World War Two, but to the man in the street during the middle and late Thirties, there were few signs of a storm gathering.

However, there were several pointers as to what could happen as the decade saw a number of international skirmishes and wars of greater or lesser importance. Wars between Italy and Abyssinia, and between Japan and China suggest that the mood for conflict was in the air. In Europe, the three-year-old Spanish Civil War was still raging in early 1939, Madrid having suffered its first air-raid on August 6, 1936. There may even have been some signs here of future events as both Germany and Italy provided military assistance to the Spanish war and there was political interference from the Soviet Union on one side and, as recent – almost unbelievable – evidence has shown, Britain on the side of the fascist, Franco!

Earlier, in 1933, Hindenburg had appointed a new Chancellor, Adolf Hitler, and by the end of February had seen the Reichstag set on fire. The following year, with Hindenburg's death, Hitler became dictator. On May 12, 1937, King George VI was crowned and May 28 saw the formation of a coalition Ministry under Neville Chamberlain.

In 1938, Germany marched into Austria. By September 26, the threat of war must have seemed very real to what the *Daily Express*

The 'W'-type Bedford, introduced in 1934, which became the benchmark for medium-sized commercials for many years. It featured semi-forward control with the centre-line of the engine over the front axle, giving a much better load distribution and a shorter vehicle, overall, for a given deck-length.

described as, "...thousands of peace-loving men and women of Britain", some of whom were engaged in digging trenches in Hyde Park! However, on September 29, the Munich ("peace in our time") Agreement was signed by Chamberlain, Daladier, Hitler and Mussolini, so all seemed well. Less than a year later, on September 3, 1939, Britain declared war on Germany, following the invasion of Poland.

In spite of all this warlike activity during the Thirties, there had been few outwardly visible signs to show that any effort was being made to ensure that the British Army was up-to-date and ready for the task of a modern war. On the civilian transport scene there was, as ever, much activity as new ideas were developed, tried out and either accepted or forgotten. Different modes of transport were still competing for supremacy: coastal shipping and inland waterways remained very active and the railways had not yet been nationalized so continued to exhibit vestiges of efficiency. On the roads in Britain, diesel engines – then known as 'oilers' – had been introduced for the heavier vehicles in the early Thirties, but most lorries remained petrol-driven and there was still a fair proportion of heavy goods traffic served by steam wagons.

Electric vehicles for goods were common in towns, and not just for milk and bread-floats; Harrods, London's famous department store, even made their own. Electricity for transport could also be seen, for passenger traffic, in the form of trolleybuses and trams as well as trains on the new commuter services. Live horsepower was still widely used for milk and coal deliveries and Carter Paterson – which, after nationalization became the backbone of British Road

Services Parcels – operated large numbers of horse-drawn vehicles. In fact, as late as 1947, over 1,850 horse-drawn vehicles were included in the fleet which was nationalized.

In a contemporary textbook several pages are devoted to arguing the merits and demerits of forward control – with the driver sitting alongside or above the engine so that no bonnet is required – and normal control – which required the vehicle to have a bonnet – so even fairly fundamental issues relating to design were still far from being fixed or finalized. Equally, the same book treats four-wheel drive (4wd) as a novelty so, as will be seen, against the background of civilian commercials, the forward-control 4wd Bedford QL 3-tonner was a remarkable product for its time.

In the mid-Thirties a new, premium quality 3-ton lorry would have cost an operator around £550 to £600, excluding tyres which, because they were seen as being consumables, were still quoted separately. The driver's wages would have been about £170 to £180 per year – about £3.50 per week. Together, insurance premiums and Road Tax amounted to about £50 and, with petrol at 1/4½d a gallon, its running costs, converted to decimal money, would have been just over 2p per mile, of which less than half was fuel!

A QLD from the very first production batch, photographed whilst on driver training. Note the central strip on the radiator mesh and the circular Bedford badge, indicative of 1941 production. Note also the 'gas-plate' beneath the driver's side of the windscreen: this was coated with a special paint which changed colour upon exposure to poisonous gas.

These two photographs of what was the author's vehicle show the condition in which some surviving QLs can be found – after nearly 50 years! The 9-ton bridge plate on the offside wing suggests that a light trailer may have been towed by this vehicle when in service. The insignia represents 3 Inf Div and the number-plate is one in the series of 'VSV' numbers issued to ex-Army vehicles upon 'demob'.

YOU–*AND* NATIONAL SERVICE

What we know as we go to Press

Lots of our folk have been asking what they ought to do in reply to the appeal made by the Government.

Well, you have all had the booklet and so have been able to study reservations and non-reservations. But it isn't quite so easy as that, because all sorts of people have individual questions to ask which are not answered in that booklet.

For "Up Above" they seek Pilots, Observers, Navigators and Wireless Operators.

For "Down Below" they seek Cooks, Bakers, Butchers and Upholsterers.

And then there are the Women's Auxiliary Services.

Now for a word about answers to inquiries.

There is an inquiry Office at

THIS EVENING

A Mass Meeting

about

NATIONAL SERVICE

in the

Winter Assembly Rooms Waller Street

at **7.30**

(Vauxhall Orchestra will play from 7.0 o'clock)

The Speakers will be

A. T. LENNOX BOYD, Esq.

M.P. for Mid-Beds and Parliamentary Secretary to the Minister of Labour

Mrs. REID-JAMIESON

Regional Officer for Women's Voluntary Services

and

A. G. WHITE, Esq., J.P., C.C.

Supported by

The Lord Lieutenant of Bedfordshire

The Rt. Hon. Lord Luke of Pavenham, K.B.E.

and others

Chairman : The Mayor of Luton

Please attend and learn more about our responsibilities

Typical of announcements appearing in the press in early 1939 when war seemed inevitable, these National Service announcements which appeared in *The Vauxhall Mirror*, aimed to keep the workforce fully informed, and went on to give details of opening times of the local Enquiry Office and other useful information.

Bedford's price list offered a range of vehicles amongst which was a 3 to 4-ton 'long' (13ft 1in) wheelbase lorry, the dropside version of which qualified for the £30 per annum road tax bracket. Prices were a mere £280 for the chassis only, £305 for the chassis/cab, £330 for the dropside lorry (painted in primer) and £434 for the 1,000cu ft capacity 'Mammoth Furniture Pantechnicon'. These prices were very attractive compared with other offerings, most of which were either much heavier or in the 2-ton bracket. The pantechnicon, especially, looks cheap by today's standards, but so too was the furniture which would have filled it. Even in the highest quality London stores, a complete bedstead could still be bought for as little as £2.10.0d and a bedroom chair for 15 shillings.

On the military side, in the late Thirties, many of the Army's vehicles in the 30cwt and 3-ton categories were relics of the previous war or else bore a strong resemblance to their civilian counterparts. Some had, as a concession to their military role, open cabs with, perhaps, a canvas canopy. Others wore cross-country tyres even though their cross-country ability must have been a little dubious. Vehicles like the six-wheeled, 4wd 30cwt Morris Commercial CDFW which entered service with the Army as late as 1934 still looked like something left over from World War One. Similarly, the heavier Leyland Retriever 6x4 3-tonner made little concession to modern thinking and, indeed, there is scant evidence of any new designs entering service between 1935 and 1939. However, parts of the War Department had been busy and, in fact, had been showing an interest in various improved transport vehicles, including multi-wheel-drive vehicles – an interest dating back long before the Bedford name came on the scene.

In November 1927, Captain C H Kuhne, RASC, speaking to the Institution of Automobile Engineers, presented a paper in which he outlined the Army's requirements and, at the same time, gave an account of progress since World War One's subsidy scheme. He referred to an earlier paper, presented in 1925 by his predecessor Captain R K Hubbard, in which was reported the formulation of "...desirable technical features...which originated in a W.D. Specification, in 1923".

The Army was looking for:

Lower intensity of pressure on the ground
Increased useful load capacity
High speed
Higher torque/weight ratio
Greater powers of adhesion to make use of the tractive effort
    available
Increased flexibility in construction, giving ability to traverse rough
    ground without setting up undue stresses in the chassis
Reasonable first cost
Economy in running and maintenance
Attractiveness to the commercial user at home, as well as in the
    Dominions and Colonies

Ease of handling
Ability to cross country without making the ground traversed more
    difficult for following vehicles

For security reasons it was not until November 1945 that the Institution heard anything further from the military on this topic. Brigadier K M F Hedges then presented a paper which included not only a full specification of the QL, but of all the other 4x4 vehicles used by the Allies during the conflict. Here he made reference to the – by then – late *Colonel* Kuhne's 1927 paper which had publicized the specification the Army was looking for and, whilst 1927 seems a long time before the war actually started it was in fact only 12 years away.

What is clear, though, is that in early 1939, the Army had a wide variety of vehicles, including straightforward 3-ton lorries; they did have four-wheel-drive vehicles – notably gun tractors of about 1932 vintage which were built by the British FWD Lorry Company at its Slough factory. They even had forward-control vehicles such as, from 1935-36, the AEC Marshal (a 6x4 3-tonner), as well as offerings by Guy, Crossley and others, so there was little that was intrinsically innovative – from the military viewpoint – about Bedford's 3-tonner. Yet this extraordinary vehicle went on to be produced in greater numbers than any of its competitors, and to survive in such numbers as to be described as "the ubiquitous QL". Certainly, many people having only a marginal interest in vehicles would, if asked to describe a World War Two 'Army lorry', describe the QL.

It was as late as 1931 that the American General Motors Corporation, which owned Vauxhall Motors of Luton, Bedfordshire, offered its first commercial vehicle for sale badged as a Bedford. This is often – mistakenly – considered to be no more than a dressed-up Chevrolet – which Vauxhall had been assembling from about 1928 – but was, in fact, an entirely new vehicle. This first Bedford – ignoring the 1914 Vauxhall, with a body described as *Bedford* – was a 2-tonner, offered with two wheelbase options: the WHG with 131in wheelbase, and the WLG with 157in. These models were the forerunners of what was to become Britain's most widely-used commercial vehicle marque. This happened, coincidentally, in the same year that the Standard Motor Company, together with their main coachbuilder, Swallow Coachworks, launched the Standard Swallow touring car. This later became known simply as the SS and was followed by the introduction of a sportier model, the SS Jaguar. Both the Bedford and the Jaguar had a six-cylinder engine, offered lots of rugged performance at a reasonable price and went on to typify the quality of the British automotive industry. Sadly, neither has survived under its original ownership.

By the outbreak of war, Bedfords accounted for one in four commercial vehicle registrations in the home market, over a third (36 per cent), in the 1½ to 3-ton payload category, and nearly half of all truck exports. Yet how did Vauxhall in general and Bedford in particular, become involved with four-wheel-drive vehicles?

Having set up in the UK in 1931, Bedford had no specific experience of producing vehicles for the War Department but, of course, Vauxhall had, having produced the 25hp staff car during World War One. Moreover, Bedford had established themselves quickly in the UK by producing a tough lorry, with a good engine, at a sensible price. They were not afraid of introducing new models either – an attribute which must have stood them in good stead during the selection process.

The earliest reference to four-wheel drive by Bedford is in the minutes of a War Office meeting held on December 23, 1938, where an engineer from Vauxhall inquired whether the War Department might be interested in such a vehicle. Not until Tuesday, September 12, 1939, nine days after the war had started, was any further mention made, this time simply to the effect that such a vehicle was "not yet required". A fortnight later events had really taken shape. The Government had given the go-ahead and on Tuesday, September 26, 1939, authorization was given for materials, procurement for the project, on a priority basis. On Thursday, October 12, only 13 working days later, a preliminary specification was submitted to the War Department – and accepted.

On Thursday, November 16, Vauxhall's Chief Engineer issued an instruction by memo, stating: "...no work of any description whatever is to be allowed to interfere with the carrying out of all work necessary in the development of the four-wheel-drive vehicle." Less than 16 weeks later, on February 1, 1940, the pilot model, QL-1, was 'on the road'.

Work on all civilian models ceased on February 6, even production of the recently introduced Model O coming to a halt when the lines were switched to production for Government contracts, not only for the QL, but also for the MW, OX and OY models. Bedford built vehicles for Government contracts from 1940 until the cessation of hostilities in 1945 and, in addition to the models already mentioned, Vauxhall Motors built many others for the War Department, amounting to nearly a quarter of a million vehicles in all, ranging from staff cars and light vans up to the famous Queen Mary articulated lorries for transporting aircraft and aircraft assemblies. A pamphlet, issued by Bedford Vehicles in 1944, and bearing the legend NOT TO BE PUBLISHED, lists no less than 45 models supplied to the Ministry of War Transport under Government contracts. They also designed and produced a new tank – the Churchill – of which 5,640 were built, and not content with that, the Luton press-shop turned out parts for some 5 million 5-gallon jerricans for carrying petrol, parts for rocket projectiles, armour piercing shells and even, during one rush period, three-quarters of a million steel helmets!

On February 28, 1940, two more QLs, vehicles QL-2 and QL-3, were submitted to the Mechanisation Experimental Establishment for testing. Both of these were of the General Service Cargo type – later to be designated QLD – and were allocated War Department

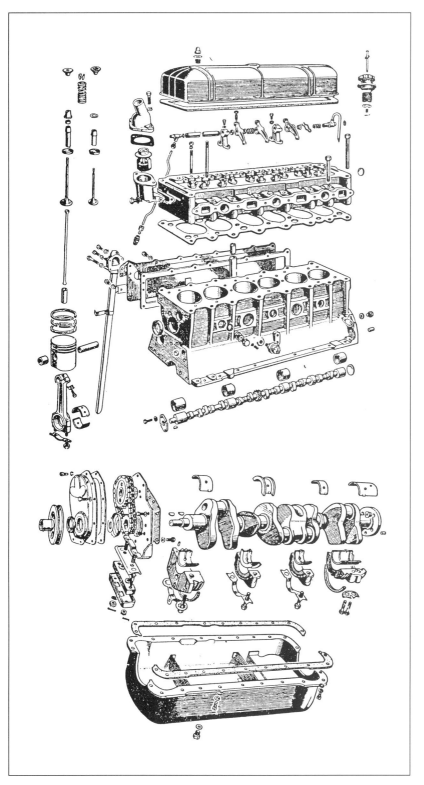

An exploded view of the Bedford 28hp engine of which over 400,000 were made, thus contributing enormously to the War Department's objective of standardization as far as was possible. Standardization also had its downside, though: the same engine was used to power both the MWD with its 15cwt payload and the QLC artic which grossed nearly 11 tons!

Census Numbers with an 'L' prefix, denoting that they were in the '3 tons and over' load capacity category. The numbers were L4182772 and L4182773. The prototype, QL-1, was not allocated a Census Number and was retained as Bedford's test-bed vehicle until it was, presumably, scrapped.

Teams of test drivers, driving day and night in all sorts of terrain and under all sorts of conditions, rapidly put many thousands of endurance test miles on the clock and, whilst apprentices were strictly forbidden to drive the new vehicles, with such a new and interesting one available, this regulation was widely flaunted. There is a story of one apprentice who managed to run over the foreman's desk, and of another who turned over a brand-new vehicle by over-exuberant application of steering lock at speed on its way to be tested. The ability to overturn unladen QLs if cornered too fast remained, throughout their life, one of their – less endearing – features.

Official stability trials, together with various braking and many other tests and trials were conducted mainly in the Luton area and on Dunstable Downs, not only on the basic vehicle, but also on the enhancements. Waterproofing tests were carried out in Wardown Park, Luton, and the winch which featured on the QLB and later on the QLW, was tested on a steep hill on the Downs.

The method of testing the winch was simple but effective. The test vehicle was anchored at the top of a steep hill whilst winching up one or more vehicles loaded with concrete blocks. The anchors consisted of mild-steel plates about 3ft long and 4in wide with four or five 1in holes drilled in them. These 'anchors' were attached to the vehicle under test by hawsers, and were fixed to the ground by driving 3ft long steel rods through the holes. A heavy-duty Avery

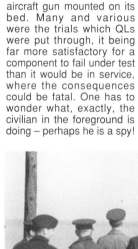

A day at the acceptance trials with the Royal Air Force; this QLC has an anti-aircraft gun mounted on its bed. Many and various were the trials which QLs were put through, it being far more satisfactory for a component to fail under test than it would be in service, where the consequences could be fatal. One has to wonder what, exactly, the civilian in the foreground is doing – perhaps he is a spy!

weigh-scale was 'in circuit' between the test vehicle and its load and the 'pull' was simply read from the dial.

Even the roof hatch in the cab underwent testing, to ensure that the hip-ring could actually take a machine-gun and, so the story goes, during testing with an Oerlikon, near Sheerness, the gun jammed in the firing position. The tester, somewhat alarmed, ducked down in the cab whilst the gun went on firing, slowly traversing the whole perimeter of the hatch completely out of control and sending-off live rounds of ammunition in all directions until the magazine was exhausted, much to the consternation of the observers.

There must be many tales emanating from the Luton factory, some of which are hard to believe, but all of which indicate the affection with which the vehicle is remembered. One such concerns the usefulness of the hand throttle whilst climbing hills. So sedately did QLs climb steep hills that apparently it was possible for the driver to leave the vehicle slowly climbing the hill, on hand throttle, whilst he attended to a call of nature behind a hedge!

A report on the Chevrolet GS truck, now in the Public Records Office, refers to the general performance of Bedfords in an indirect way when it states: "...its petrol consumption is better than that of all other trucks tested except the Bedford, which was outstanding in this respect."

When both Bedford and the Farnborough, Hampshire-based WVEE (Wheeled Vehicle Experimental Establishment – forerunner of the FVRDE, the Fighting Vehicles Research and Development Establishment at Chobham, Surrey), were satisfied that enough was enough, the two test vehicles were completely stripped down and examined in minute detail. Very few modifications were required, one being that the chassis crossmembers were showing signs of fatigue in two places near the transfer gearbox. The design was changed to add more metal at the points which looked as though they might fail and some modifications were made to the braking system. Prototyping and testing were then, more or less, complete.

Indicative of the lengths to which testing was taken, this shot shows a Bedford 4x2 3-ton Model OY mobile X-Ray laboratory wading in five feet of water. To prevent the vehicle from floating – undesirable because without its wheels on the bottom it had no means of propulsion, unlike the DUKWs – the rear door was left open! Inside, all vulnerable equipment was carefully stowed in watertight containers and the front generator compartment was completely sealed. Bedford built over 72,000 OYs on WD contracts.

In February 1941, the QL went into series production in earnest. The Army was, by then, desperately short of vehicles, many hundreds of all types, including requisitioned civilian vehicles, having been lost at Dunkirk in May and June, 1940. The retreat from Dunkirk was seen by some in authority as a blessing in disguise, at least insofar as Army transport was concerned. It had the effect of clearing out at one go all the miscellaneous and aged vehicles which had been accumulated from many different manufacturers and which had, therefore, widely differing specifications. One of the reasons that Bedford went on to build such huge numbers of vehicles during the war was because of the opportunities this gave for standardization – the ultimate aim of many fleet operators, and especially of the military. This led, as will be seen, to having some strange anomalies of over and underpowering by using the same engine specification throughout the weight range.

WEEKLY VEHICLE RECORD

Form Z/F/5A

Vehicle No...........................

Fuel used *Petrol.* / *Diesel Oil.* (*Strike out whichever does not apply*).

Unladen Weight...........................

Group No...........................

One Sheet is to be used for each vehicle for each rationing week. The sheet is to be handed to the Group Organiser on the day following the last day of each rationing week.

Date.	Journey*		Miles			Description of Goods carried	Fuel used Gallons
	From	To	Loaded over 50 per cent. capacity	Loaded under 50 per cent. capacity	Empty		

Date...........................

Certified that the above is a true record.

* In the case of circular journeys, intermediate points sufficient to identify the journey taken should be given, e.g. journey from A to A via B, C and D.

....
Signature of Operator.

W. Cannings, 23-25 Peckham High Street, S.E.1.A.

Form ZF/5/A was issued to civilian operators so that the authorities could assess their utilization and availability for other work. A form had to be completed for every vehicle, every week, and the bureaucracy entailed can only be guessed at!

29

CHAPTER 3

QL

The official War Department description of the Bedford QL was 'Lorry, 3-ton, 4x4, Bedford'. Its extremely functional appearance, with the sloping flat front and high ground clearance, makes it, almost certainly, the man-in-the-street's idea of a World War Two Army lorry. It was also one of the most popular vehicles with the men who had to drive it and, even to those who did not have what many consider to be that pleasure and privilege, its characteristic sound – partly engine noise, partly tyre noise but, mostly, the amazing whine from the gears in the four-wheel-drive transfer case – were both comforting and endearing. It might even be claimed that the QL is unique in military vehicle history, if only for the sentiments it still arouses over 50 years after work started on its design. Whilst not as noisy as the Austin K5, whose mechanical symphony could be heard a very long way off, earning it the *nom de guerre* of 'The Screamer', the Bedford QL did have a similarly distinctive sound and, to many who were not amongst the *cognoscenti* of military vehicles, it, too, was a Screamer.

Bedford produced a total of 554,865 vehicles for the War Department between 1930 and 1948 and, for the war years alone, they built an astonishing total of 215,258 vehicles. The 52,000-odd QLs thus represented a fraction under a quarter of their total wartime production. Figures for annual production are given below:

Vauxhall Motors Ltd wartime production figures

Year	Total vehicles produced	Percentage QLs
1941	40,983	9.3
1942	48,948	19.9
1943	50,814	24.5
1944	35,740	33.7
1945	38,773	36.6

Spurlings provided many bodies for Bedfords, of all types, during the war years, as well as many bodies for other makes. They also retained their Bedford interests long after the war, as this postwar aerial view of their main facility shows. Note that Leyland and BMC models are lined-up as well as Bedfords.

The exact number of QLs produced between 1940 and 1945, including Vauxhall's prototype which was retained at the Bedford works as a test bed, was 52,248. The production figures in each year are shown in the next table. The 1940 figures are for the two vehicles, whose chassis numbers were 1001 and 1002, which were the War Department's prototypes, and were used for testing and acceptance trials. Also, QL-1, Vauxhall's own prototype, is included, which may not have been given a chassis number as it never left Vauxhall's possession but, equally, may have been given the chassis number 1000.

Annual production of QLs *

Year	Chassis numbers Start	Finish	Engine numbers Start	Finish	Total produced
1940	1,000	1,002	?	?	3
1941	1,003	4,795	2,001	6,314	3,793
1942	4,796	14,555	6,315	16,403	9,760
1943	14,556	26,998	16,404	32,692	12,443
1944	26,999	39,051	32,693	45,829	12,053
1945	39,052	53,247	45,830	61,648	14,196

* Bedford: Engineering Records Dept. (ERD), (except 1940).

The figures provided by Bedford's Engineering Records Department (ERD) pose something of a puzzle. The annual figures fail to tally with those used by the War Department and, in fact, it is not at all clear what the ERD were doing in keeping track of production in this way. Their normal function was to keep all the drawings, specifications, dates of release to production, and allocation and control of use of part numbers. They also produced the parts lists that were used all over the factory so it was certainly not part of their usual duties to track production numbers. Moreover, the War Department figures in the next table are actually higher than those issued by the factory, so the age-old practice of registering vehicles before they left the factory – or even before they were made! – to boost the figures in the monthly New Vehicle Registrations so as to be higher than those of competitors, does not appear to apply. In wartime there seems to be little point in such a fiddle anyway so the probable explanation is that the official, War Department, figures relate to orders placed – and hence to the Census Numbers which were allocated – and the ERD numbers relate to orders fulfilled by the factory.

WD records: QLs by year

| | Chassis numbers | | Year | Cumul | Cumul |
	Start	Finish	total	total	total (ERD)
1941	1,001	7,229	6,229	6,229	3,793
1942	7,230	18,161	10,392	17,161	13,553
1943	18,162	30,340	12,179	29,340	25,996
1944	30,341	42,121	11,781	41,121	38,049
1945	42,122	53,247	11,126	52,247	52,245

Precise details of which models were produced, in what numbers and in which years, are no longer available from factory records, but with the aid of surviving details from the original contracts placed with Bedford, it is possible to make the following arithmetical deductions:

Estimated annual model production: 1940-45 (*a*) (*b*)

Model	1940	1941	1942	1943	1944	1945	Total
QLB	–	1,269	774	1,859	816	782	5,500
QLC	–	1,914	2,347	902	404	1,374	6,941
QLD(*c*)	3	2,224	4,446	6,666	7,318	5,047	25,704
QLR	–	766	2,174	2,406	1,698	1,739	8,783
QLT	–	54	1,191	346	1,545	237	3,373
QLW	–	–	–	–	–	1,947	1,947
Total	3	6,227	10,932	12,179	11,781	11,126	52,248

a)Arithmetical deductions only.

b)The year total for 1941 (6,227) disagrees with the previous table in which 1940 production is included with 1941's. The Bedford prototype is not usually included in the official figures.

c) 1940 includes Bedford and WD prototypes.

The Karrier Spider from which the K6 was developed, this very Thirties' design is not dissimilar to the Model CK6, 6x4 3-tonner from Karrier, of which numbers were produced in the late Thirties. Neither this model, nor the K6 itself, were produced in great quantities and this one, in particular, never really caught on.

Bedford, since their very first models in 1931, right up to the time they ceased existence as an arm of General Motors, and even beyond into new ownership with AWD in 1990 and again, under Marshall's SPV from 1993, always used a two-letter model designation to describe their vehicles, often supplemented by one or two more

letters to give a greater level of identification. In general, the model letters are not initials of anything in particular and cannot usually be interpreted. Various suggestions have been made about what QL might stand for such as: Quadruple Locomotion, Quick Loading – which they were not – or for Quad – Long wheelbase, this latter being a little more likely as the Army often referred to four-wheel-drive vehicles as 'quads' and Bedford sometimes used an L – as the third letter – to denote long wheelbases.

However, the third letter of the model designation could sometimes be interpreted and, on QLs, this is certainly the case, even if some of the interpretations are a little stretched! The interpretations are:

QLB   Bofors Light AA Tractor.
QLC   Chassis/cab – for special bodies not built by Bedford.
QLD   No direct interpretation, although Bedford had, in the
        past, used D to denote dropside which, of course, the QLD
        was not.
QLT   Trooper
QLW   Winch (the tipper version which was fitted with winch
        equipment).

The QL was not, by any means, the fastest vehicle in the British Army but, for those who drove them, it was reckoned to be amongst the best pullers, even with only 72bhp (brake horsepower) available.

The Karrier K6 was the 4x4 offering from what became the Rootes Group – Humber: Hillman: Singer: Sunbeam Talbot: Commer: Karrier. This model is fitted with the No.5 General Service body and was equipped to APT speci-fication. It was also fitted with a vertical spindle winch just in front of the rear axle. A non-winch equipped version was also available, which allowed the body to be mounted rather lower, but this necessitated cutting out wheelarches.

Power was supplied by Bedford's so-called WD Type engine which the RAC rated as 27.34hp. This led to endless confusion and the engine was often, wrongly, known as the '27hp' engine. The colloquial name, 'twenty-seven horse' applied to the old RAC 26.3hp version of the Bedford engine; the newer WD Type, introduced in 1937-38, was more properly known as the '28hp', rounding up from the RAC rating of 27.34! To make matters worse, there is also often confusion about the difference between RAC horsepower and brake horsepower. RAC horsepower is calculated from a formula which takes into account the bore and stroke of the engine as well as the number of cylinders, so is simply related to engine capacity. On the other hand, brake horsepower is a measure of engine output, measured on a device which incorporates a brake which tries to stall the engine at full power.

The Bedford's 72bhp was developed at an engine speed of 3,000rpm which gave the vehicle a design top speed of 48mph. However, all of the early and nearly all of the later models were governed down to 2,500rpm, reducing the power output to 68bhp and the top speed to 38mph. This still left plenty in hand as the recommended convoy speed for QLs was 25mph! Resourceful soldiers, of course, found ways to exceed these limits, either by illegally fiddling with the governor – a risky procedure as the evidence was there to be seen – or, where circumstances allowed, by use of 'Mexican overdrive': coasting down hills in neutral, which was great fun until the brakes became too hot to be useful!

Of the 400,000 engines built to the WD specification by Bedford, some 250,000 were installed in 'special' military vehicles to the order of the Ministry of Supply. They differed from the normal civilian product only in that they were fitted with Solex carburettors and 12-volt electrics instead of Zenith carburettors and a 6-volt system.

Whilst 72bhp is not at all unreasonable for a vehicle whose all-up weight should not have exceeded 7½ tons, it must be confessed that, laden, performance could be decidedly unexciting on occasions. Perhaps the alleged difference in attitudes of the British and the American military authorities towards vehicle power were responsible. If the vehicle designers calculate that a vehicle needs a 100bhp engine, the American attitude is said to err on the safe side so an engine of 200bhp is installed. The British authorities, by contrast, err on the cheap side, and install a 50bhp unit! However, it seems that any shortcomings in raw power were more than compensated by the excellent matching of the gearbox to the engine which, in any case, was very reliable.

In a similar form, the engine had, after all, sold in huge quantities to the British civilian market between 1931 and 1939. It had been developed by improving an even longer-standing Chevrolet design so was, indeed, a tried and proven unit. With a compression ratio of only 6.22:1, enabling it to run on very low-octane fuels – sometimes as low as 80 – and the 'long-stroke' characteristic of the engine, the QL's power unit was a very flexible piece of equipment capable of performing arduous tasks over long periods. A 'long-stroke characteristic' simply means that the piston-stroke dimension is greater than the cylinder-bore dimension, which tends to give a very 'torquey' engine, requiring less gear-changing and having very good 'lugging' power; if the relationship between the dimensions is reversed the result is an 'oversquare' engine which, typically, needs higher revs to attain its power.

Low-octane fuels are no longer available in Britain and those QLs which have survived into preservation today have to contend with 4-star petrol – unleaded is totally unsuitable – and, to avoid damage to the engine, this must be diluted with 1:20 of diesel fuel. Paraffin does the job just as well, but is not strictly legal as no Excise Duty has been paid on it.

Transmission was via a 10in single-dry-plate clutch to a four-speed, crash gearbox which was first introduced in civilian models in 1934 and, with minor changes only – including some which were made specially for military vehicles – continued in production until 1951 when it was superseded by a synchromesh gearbox. B Thomas, formerly with REME, tells how some drivers would delight in their ability to change gear silently with the crash-box, without using the clutch. Changing gear up the box is not too difficult, if your timing is right, but it is a little more tricky getting it right when changing down! The main gearbox transmitted drive to a transfer box which contained high and low ratios and the four-wheel-drive gears, engagement of low ratio automatically bringing in the four-wheel drive. First gear, even in the high-ratio range, is a very low gear and was rarely used, even for hill-starts, when the vehicle was unladen. First gear in the low-ratio, 4wd, range is a prodigiously low gear and gives the vehicle its 'go-absolutely-anywhere' characteristic.

The QL's axles were of the fully floating type, meaning that the wheel hub is carried on bearings – two in the case of the QL – located on the outside of the axle casing. The halfshafts thus transmit drive only, with all the weight of the vehicle being taken by the axle casing. Also, the outer ends of the halfshafts carried flanges secured to the wheel hubs by studs, this having the advantage that in the event of a halfshaft breaking, the broken pieces could be removed without jacking-up the vehicle and, with the sound halfshaft from the other side also removed, the vehicle could be towed, still laden. This later became common practice on most vehicles but was innovative in the Thirties, only being applied to heavier vehicles where an additional margin of safety was required.

An interesting feature which first appeared on the QL is the large flanges on the hubs. Presented by the War Department with the problem of devising a quick and efficient way of loading vehicles into ships, Vauxhall's designers worked on the principle that the most sensible place to support a vehicle was where it was usually supported – at the axles. Howard W Holding, one of the Vauxhall engineers responsible for chassis development between 1933 and 1948, came up with the idea of fitting an enlarged disc to the hub-ends so that slings, suspended from a spreader, could quickly and simply lift the vehicle aloft. On later versions, both the flange and the hub itself were knurled – to provide a better grip on the slings and a foot grip when used as a step-up into the cab. The rear flanges did not need knurling as they were not used as steps, so were simply constructed from a flat piece of ¼in thick sheet, suitably drilled to take the hub nuts.

The Ford WOT6 in its 'Machy', or Machinery Workshop guise. Many Fords were used in this role and also for Breakdown Gantries, although neither role was adopted by QLs in any great number, for some reason. In service the body interior would be packed with work-benches, lathes and other equipment, and bench-vices were bolted to the folding sides so that, in the lowered position, the 'flaps' also acted as work-benches.

Many innovations were incorporated into the design of the QL, and during the five years of its production, several new ideas were built-in as improvements. One of the innovations concerns the fuel-tank cap which, by any standards, is large – for a very strange reason. During the initial design stages, Bedford's designers had come up with a number of options for the eventual component, all having one or another advantage. Officials at the War Department would not take a decision based just on the engineers' drawings and insisted on seeing them 'in real life'. Prototypes were duly made up and the Top Brass invited to a demonstration at Luton. Inevitably, one of their number was delayed so the remainder decided to go for lunch with the intention of seeing the demonstration in the afternoon. Alcohol was consumed during lunch and, when it came to trying to pour a can full of petrol into the tank, this enormous opening was the only one they could manage!

Whilst on the subject of fuel and fuel tanks, two different specifications, single or twin-tank, were available depending upon the model. Each had its own emergency reserve system which it was well worth remembering; it is never particularly funny to run out of petrol but to do so in wartime is especially unamusing! The Army procedure, on twin-tank versions, was to draw on the right-hand tank first, switching to the left-hand, reserve, tank when that ran out. This was done by pushing in the tap on top of the tank to draw on the reserve – its normal (right-hand tank) position being pulled out. Also, on the left-hand tank, there was another tap giving access to a last-resort reserve of about 4 gallons and, to reach this, the tap on the left-hand tank had to be pulled out. It was much simpler on the single-tank versions! Push-in to shut off fuel altogether; pull-out to switch on the fuel; pull-out a little further and twist to obtain the reserve of about 4 gallons. Refuellers were instructed to ensure that all reserve taps were returned to their correct positions each time the vehicle was refuelled.

Very few fundamental modifications were made to the basic QL design during its years of production, even though certain 'extras' were added to the specification, as the war progressed. For some unrecorded reason – probably a niggardly attempt to save materials – the vertical strip down the centre of the radiator mesh was discontinued as was the original circular Bedford badge featuring the Griffin, which was replaced by a small rectangular piece of steel with Bedford stamped on it. This is an immediate giveaway for preserved vehicles where owners tend to exaggerate the age of their vehicle and, whilst the exact date of the change is not known precisely, all of the 1941 and some of the 1942 production had the central radiator strip and the circular badge featuring the Griffin. Some very early production versions did not have the flanged hubs, even though the prototypes did, and the AA hip-ring was also not fitted on some of the earliest production. Later in the war came the requirement for QLs to be built to air-portable (APT – a strange acronym!) specification enabling them to be carried almost ckd (completely knocked down) in Dakota aircraft. The very latest version, still being produced when the war ended, was made to APT specification and was also 'tropicalized', embodying certain modifications to, amongst other things, the cooling system, for use after victory in Europe.

Other modifications were made at various times for application in

The Albion model FT11N bore a very strong visual resemblance to the more-or-less contemporary civilian offering from this Scottish company in the 3 tons payload category. Compared with the QL, very few of these – only about 1,000 – were built.

different theatres of the war. An example of this is when all hands from the apprentice school were called-out to work overtime, one Saturday, fitting replacement rubber seals to the brake cylinders on a large batch of QLs destined for Russia. These were needed because the freezing temperatures would have cracked the seals and rendered the brakes useless.

The QL was not the only 4x4 3-tonner available to the armed forces although it was by far the most numerous. Albion, Austin, Crossley, Ford, Karrier and Thornycroft all had vehicles in this category and there were also offerings from both Canada and the USA. In Canada, Ford and Chevrolet produced large numbers of 4x4 3-tonners of the famous CMP (Canadian Military Pattern) design. American production tended to opt for greater horsepowers and their offerings in this category were, in fact, rated for 4 tons. Oddly, their 3-ton models were usually Chevrolet or Dodge six-wheelers, with four-wheel drive, having normal or semi-forward control. Their 4x4 4-tonners were mainly FWD and GMC with some Autocars and Federals as well.

In Britain, Albion Motors, of Glasgow, produced a military version of their civilian Model 127 with, of course, the addition of four-wheel drive. Known as the Model FT11N, it first appeared about February 1940, and about 1,000 of them were produced from 1941 onwards. Apart from the FT11N and a 3-ton 6x6, Albion concentrated on heavier models, including 10-ton 6x4s and tank transporters, of which about 1,000 were built, as well as an 8x8 prototype. The FT11N was fitted with Albion's own engine, the 4,560cc Type EN280A, which was a side-valve, six-cylinder petrol engine developing 90bhp. The transmission arrangements were much the same as the QL except for the added sophistication of a lockable differential – very modern for its day! In appearance, the FT11N was not dissimilar to the QL but had a perpendicular scuttle and steeply sloping windscreen.

Austin's offering was the 3-ton 4x4 Type K5. At the outbreak of war, Austin were already producing a military 3-tonner, the K3, which was a 6x2 available with several body options and a 'soft-top' cab. In 1940 the K3 was uprated to 6x4 and the model was eventually replaced by the K6 in 1944. Austin also produced the famous *Katy*, the K2 30cwt which was the Army's staple ambulance chassis. Production of 4x4s, in any quantity, did not start until 1941 so the 6x4 K3 was kept on and used throughout the war years. The missing number, K4, did not appear until 1952, as the civilian Loadstar model. A short wheelbase, 4x4 military variant of this was made available as the K9.

Broadly similar to the QL, the K5 differed in having servo-assistance to the brakes rather than vacuum-hydraulics. Its engine was a six-cylinder, 3,995cc ohv unit developing 85bhp. Supplied as GS (General Service), or as a 6-pounder A T Portee, more or less identical to the QL version, some 12,280 were produced between 1941 and 1945. The K5, which was 19ft 8in long and 7ft 3in wide, was easily identifiable by having a perpendicular scuttle and a

The Thornycroft Nubian, one of the earlier 3-tonners to become available in four-wheel drive, and another which was not produced in very great numbers, some 4,000 or so being put into service.

perpendicular windscreen, giving a very flat-front appearance. The brush-bar was also mounted lower than on the QL.

The Crossley was very similar in general appearance to the Austin K5, except that the radiator grille was less obtrusive. Until the war started, the RAF was responsible for its own vehicle procurement and the Crossley Q Type, which was more popular with the RAF than with the Army, was well represented. Crossleys were the first of the 4x4s in production, entering service in mid-1940, but their specification reflected their ancestry, going back into the early and mid-Thirties (but not as 4x4s). They were fitted with their own 5,266cc side-valve Type 30/100 engine which developed 90bhp from only four cylinders. Brakes had servo-assistance and there was a vacuum system fitted for use with a trailer, for the Crossley was often used as the tractor unit for the Queen Mary aircraft trailers, a role for which it was well suited because of its shorter wheelbase. It was also available with GS Cargo, flat-bed, fire-tender and ballast bodies, as well as box-bodies for office types. Its dimensions were 20ft 3in long, 7ft 6in wide and, in box-body form, exactly 11ft high. About 11,000 were produced during the war years.

Competition from the Ford stable was in the shape of the Model WOT6 which, after Bedford and Austin, was the next most numerous of the 4x4s. Its mechanical specification was markedly different from the others for it boasted a V8 engine, but of only 3,621cc – relatively small for a V8 – and it was side-valve operated! Brakes were old-fashioned mechanical types, but it was nevertheless a popular vehicle pushing out masses of torque. Entering

production later than the others, in 1942, it was probably most similar to the QL in appearance and, of the 30,000 or so produced between 1942 and 1945, GS Cargo, Breakdown Gantry, Machinery Workshop and many other types were available, latterly to air-portable specification. In GS Cargo form it measured 19ft 10½in long by 7ft 6in wide and some remained in service until 1962. Ford also produced, in the same 'series', the 3-ton WOT1 which was a 6x4 version of the 4x2 WOT3, the 15cwt 4x2 WOT2 and the 30cwt WOT8. Perhaps for obvious reasons, the WOT4 designation was avoided!

From Karrier came an odd-looking contribution, the K6, which had a similar mechanical specification to most of the other makes, although some K6s were fitted with a vertical spindle winch. Its appearance differed from the others in the category in that it was of semi-forward control design, with large front wings. It was, though, one of the earlier contenders, having arrived on the scene in late 1940, and few were built. Karrier also produced, during the war years, the CK6 3-ton six-wheeler, several versions of the Bantam and a 4wd gun tractor, the KT4.

Thornycroft's 4x4 3-ton offering, one of which had been delivered to Farnborough for testing by June 6, 1940, was designated the Nubian, a name associated with Thornycroft for many years, even after the war. The Nubian, of which only about 4,000 were built, had Thornycroft's four-cylinder, 3,865cc petrol engine, the AC4/1, which developed 85bhp. In many respects, the technical details were similar to the QL but epicyclic gears were used for hub-reduction. It had a 12ft wheelbase and ran on 12 x 20in tyres. Postwar, Thornycroft concentrated more on heavier vehicles, producing the Nubian fire tenders for airport work and the Mighty Antar tank transporter.

People involved with any these vehicles seem to remember them with affection and none more so than Bedford's QL. In response to an article placed in the *Luton Citizen*, many ex-drivers and production line workers wrote to offer reminiscences. Typical is one from Jack Bingham, formerly Regimental Transport Sergeant with the 7th Hussars, who was in charge of 30 QLs in addition to various other types. He recalls the QL as a much-loved and popular vehicle with Army drivers – as were all the Bedfords. They were loved for their sturdiness and reliability, and few and far between have been the reports of mechanical faults with them.

One correspondent recalls the HT lead from the coil fracturing and being repaired, on the road, by the simple expedient of a pin! Another tells of the petrol pump packing up and being hand-worked by a fitter whilst on the move to enable them to return to base, and yet another tells of how performance was improved by a little device made from fuse-wire and a trouser button, to delay the spark! Whether true or not, clearly there are fond memories. Certainly, the 28hp engine had several endearing features, one being its tendency to develop piston-slap giving a very 'loosened-up' sound. Amongst its less endearing traits was its refusal to start if the driver was careless with the throttle. Bedford's explicit instructions were that the engine should be started by pulling out the choke, switching on the ignition, with your foot well clear of the accelerator pedal – and, of course, the hand throttle which was linked to the foot throttle rods, firmly closed – then pressing the starter. No instructions were

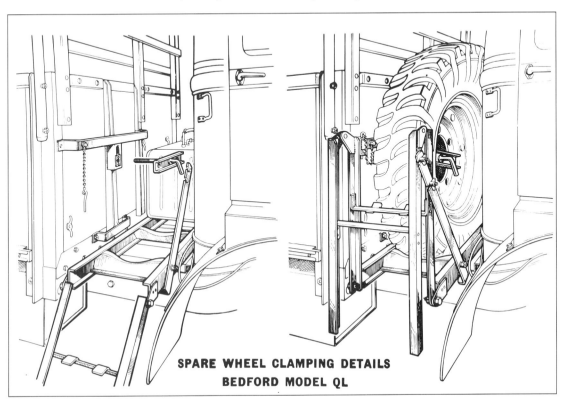

**SPARE WHEEL CLAMPING DETAILS
BEDFORD MODEL QL**

Typical views of the inside of a mobile machinery (or 'machy') workshop, showing the lathes, grinders, generators and other equipment used in the field for 'light aid'. Any, more extensive, repairs were passed back down the line to fully-equipped workshops, the ultimate step being the base workshop.

given for starting a warm engine which could, on occasion, be just as easy to flood! Another annoyance was its tendency for the starter pinion to jam in wet or damp weather – easily enough cured by a light tap on the end of the starter housing, but an annoyance, all the same.

It has already been seen that possibly the most memorable of all the QL's characteristics was its sound – which earned it the name of the Screamer, if only by mis-identification with Austin's K5. Until four-wheel drive is engaged, the gears in the transfer box revolve in neutral and it is this which made the music. Geoff Charman, formerly in the RAF with 21 Heavy AA at Formby, Liverpool, tells the story of one Saturday afternoon in the guardroom, guarding two 'prisoners' who were confined to barracks. Things had become fairly relaxed, with both prisoners and guards taking it in turns to make tea, so it was a little while until it was noticed that the three prisoners were neither imprisoned, nor making tea. Mild panic set in and all efforts were made to locate any sort of vehicle to find them, it being a good bet that they were on their way into the local town. In the event, the only one available was a QL so a group set off in hot pursuit.

The escapees, who were indeed on their way into the local town, hearing the familiar whine coming up astern, thought this might be a good vehicle in which to hitch a lift. The driver generously stopped for them, inviting them to hop in the back. They did – right into the arms of the RAF Police!

There were, of course, criticisms. One complaint relates to the spare wheel which was located behind the cab on the offside and which is held in place by a toggle bar, the whole assembly being protected by a folding frame. When unfolded the frame formed a ladder which allowed the spare to roll down. It was fine coming down, but decidedly more difficult to replace as the two-piece Sankey wheel, with its 10.5 x 20in tyre, was an extremely heavy piece of kit.

CHAPTER 4

QLB and other fighting QLs

All Army vehicles are classified into one of three general types: A, B or C. 'A' vehicles carry armour and 'do the fighting' and this group includes tanks, armoured personnel carriers, self-propelled guns and so on. 'C' vehicles are those used in construction work and include such items as bulldozers.

However, 'B' vehicles are not armoured and are much more readily identified with their civilian counterparts. The group includes lorries and buses and all those vehicles which are used for the myriad transport needs of an Army at war – everything from ambulances and canteens to recovery vehicles and water bowsers. They are frequently referred to as 'soft-skinned' and the QL was thus designated a 'B' vehicle. The 'B' classification has nothing to do with the B in QLB, this being purely Bedford's model designation.

So the Bedford QL was originally designed and developed as a logistics vehicle whose purpose was the transport of goods and people. In spite of its 'B' classification, its ruggedness and versatility soon meant that it was destined for other, non-logistic and less passive roles – if carrying ammunition to guns in the front line can be called passive! These roles were to include some tasks which were downright aggressive, foremost amongst which was the role of the QLB.

QLB Light Anti-Aircraft Gun Tractor
In common with the Morris CDSW 6x4 Tractor unit, which the QL gradually replaced, the QLB towed a Bofors 40mm Light Anti-Aircraft (or ack-ack) gun. Remaining in service throughout the war years, the QLB was, itself, ultimately replaced by the 6x6 AEC Militant as AA guns and associated equipment became generally heavier and more sophisticated.

The 'B' carried a crew of nine, with seating provided for the driver plus one crew in the cab. The remainder of the crew sat 'in the back'

The QLB Bofors LAA Gun Tractor, clearly showing all the lockers and ammunition storage boxes. The two long boxes on the bed of the vehicle are for the 40mm Bofors ammunition; immediately above them, in two groups of two, are the general kit lockers. The third box on the second row contains, on the nearside, the tool roll, wheelbraces and oil can and, on the offside, the snatch-block, shackles, hawsers and towing rope. The two tractor scotches can also clearly be seen tucked into their recesses behind the rear mudguards. The QLB is shown without the spare wheel having been fitted and without its census numbers or any legend on the yellow bridge plate. Bridge plates carried a number representing the vehicle's gross laden weight and vehicles were not permitted to cross bridges which carried a lower number than that displayed on the vehicle.

with five of them actually in the crew compartment and two more seated between the lockers in the rear. The crew compartment itself had doors on either side which were fitted with detachable side curtains, and there was a sliding panel in the roof for ventilation. To enable the vehicle to be shipped economically, both the driver's and the crew's cab tops could be removed to give a reduced shipping height of 7ft 6in thus saving 18in of space and giving a 'tonnage standing' – a term used to denote a shipping 'packing factor' – of 31.8 tons. There was little wasted space in the back of a QLB as in the rear of the body there was stacked a quantity of 40mm ammunition, in eight cases – four each side – together with all the other equipment required by a vehicle fulfilling such a role. This

included a spare gun barrel, which was stored in its case amidships, as well as a spare gun-wheel, which was stowed behind the crew compartment. The rest of the crew's personal and fighting kit and other equipment was kept in a variety of containers and lockers.

QLBs were fitted with power winches to assist with manoeuvring the trailer and for recovering itself from bogged-down positions. The winches which were supplied could be one of two types: Wild or Turner. The Wild gear is so-named simply because it was produced by M B Wild & Co. This model had angled winch-sheaves and 183ft of steel wire rope. The Turner specification was produced by The Turner Manufacturing Co, and had horizontal sheaves and 175ft of rope. In basic specification and performance they were almost identical, both having a maximum rope pull of 6 tons with the drum unwound, or 4 tons with wire wound on to the drum – the pull being less with rope wound-on because of the tendency of the rope to cut into line already on the drum. With the engine running at its maximum – governed – speed, the rope could be wound-in at the rate of 209ft per minute, so, in a hurry, both could wind-in in less than a minute, unloaded. Whilst the 'specs' were almost identical there were a couple of differences – in the reduction gear ratio, and in the gearbox oil capacity.

Bofors gun tractors on their own weighed-in at about 6 tons 12cwt with all their kit aboard, but to this had to be added the weight of the gun and its trailer, which varied depending upon exactly which version of the trailer and Mark of the gun were attached. Unladen, the vehicle weighed 4 ton 4cwt 1lb, which was distributed with 2 tons on the front axle and the remainder on the rear. The QLB was 18ft 8in long and could turn in a 54ft circle. Those QLBs which served in the Western depot were usually marked with an RAF roundel on the roof for identification purposes.

It is interesting to note how quickly the authorities caught on to

A Bofors light anti-aircraft gun and trailer as towed by the QLB and one or two other makers' offerings – notably the Austin K5. The gun fired 40mm ammunition, of which 96 rounds were carried in the body of the towing vehicle, as was the crew which, in this photo, appears to have been abandoned in a puddle! In 'transport mode' the gun barrel was carried horizontally.

the fact that what had been designed as an on/off-road load carrying vehicle for, basically, General Service Cargo work, was also eminently suitable for many other roles, including that of a light gun-tractor. In fact, the first ever production contract placed for production of QLs called for a quantity of QLBs, so clearly their suitability became apparent during the War Department's initial acceptance trials. Surviving records show the contract to be dated May 4, 1942, but there are some other references in the official records which disagree with this. Unfortunately, indeed frustratingly, dates in the records are almost always unreliable and often relate not to the date of placing the contract, but to some later addition or amendment – or even to when the card or document was filled out. That these dates are unreliable is indicated by the fact that production on the contract had already started in the first quarter of the previous year. The contract, number V3949, called for 1,771 QLB Bofors LAA together with 2,501 QLD GS, the standard General Service lorry, which is looked at in detail in Chapter 6. These first QLBs went into service numbered, incorrectly as it happens, as L4483034 to L4484804. The numbers, or at least their prefixes, are, strictly, incorrect because the QLB was a gun-tractor and should thus have had an 'H' prefix. Perhaps a brief word about military numbering would not be out of place!

From the late Thirties until after the war, all armed services vehicles were allocated a WD – or Census – Number. The numbers ran sequentially regardless of vehicle type but were prefixed with an identifying letter (which, incidentally, had nothing to do with the classification into 'A', 'B' and 'C', discussed at the start of the chapter) so, for example, ambulances were prefixed with an 'A'. 'H' was used to denote a tractor unit (or 'hauler'); 'L' was used for

The 8th Army crosses into Tunisia; this photograph was taken on the Northern Section of the coast road in mid-February 1943, and shows what was officially described as 'artillery crossing into Tunisia'. The artillery is, in fact, light anti-aircraft artillery (Bofors LAA) being towed by a fully stripped down QLB. The Italian signpost has had the Highland Division's sign added to it.

lorries whose payload capacity was 3 tons and over, and was the letter which usually applied to QLs and similar vehicles; 'M's were used on 'medium' lorries, with a payload capacity of more than 30cwt but less than 3 tons; 'T' denoted that the bearer was a tracked vehicle; 'V' stood for vans – a prefix which was rarely used – and 'Z' represented a light vehicle with a load capacity of up to 30cwt. Occasionally, a further 'C' prefix was added to denote allocation to the Canadian forces.

Most QLs had an 'L' prefix since the vehicle was defined as Lorry 3 ton 4x4. Strangely, this even applied to the QLC articulated combination (Chapter 5) since the tractor and trailer could not be separated in the way we normally think of artics; had they been separable, the tractor unit would have had an 'H' prefix.

Correctly numbered H5366221 to H5367453, another contract for QLBs is also of particular interest. Calling for a total of 1,233 vehicles, to be delivered at the rate of 120 per month from August 1943, the last of the batch was extracted and sent to the Wheeled Vehicle Experimental Establishment at Farnborough. Given WVEE reference number 1488, this became the prototype QLW (Chapter 6), the tipper version of the QL which was fitted with a winch – hence the use of the QLB chassis as the prototype. This then went into service with the Census Number L5367453.

By 1945, contracts had been placed for about 5,500 QLBs, representing more than 10 per cent of all QL production and many were, after their wartime use, converted to GS Cargo bodies.

OTHER FIGHTING QLs

6-pounder Anti-Tank Gun Portee

The 6-pounder Anti-Tank Portee, more accurately referred to as a 'Portee and Fire' vehicle, was developed to meet a need for improved mobility and flexibility for the Army's range of anti-tank weapons in the war in the desert. Built on the QLC chassis, it is quite often referred to – even in the official records – as a QLB although, for several reasons, it is unlikely that QLB chassis were ever used.

The idea of carrying the gun, rather than towing it, was not a new development and, in fact, was first tried out during World War One. One of the problems with a towed gun was its general vulnerability and lack of manoeuvrability, whereas a gun which could be mounted on the vehicle could, in today's terminology, 'shoot and scoot'. The 6-pounder field gun which formed the armament for the outfit, *could* be towed, but was much more usually carried, there being three different ways to do this.

In fighting trim, the gun could be mounted so as to fire off forwards over the canvas-top cab. To achieve this, various preparations had to be made: importantly, the radiator had to be protected and a large anti-blast plate was provided for the purpose. Firing-off this way also entailed having the cab top and sides as well as the windscreen folded down. Also, the gun-trail had to be split. With the gun in this position, the front axle weight was 3 ton 18cwt

3qtr and the rear axle's 3 ton 12cwt 2qtr, making up the total gross weight, with the gun, of 7 ton 11cwt 1qtr. Luckily, Bedfords had always been famous for their capacity to accept an overload, as their nominal maximum gross weight was 7 ton 10cwt!

The gun could also be mounted to fire off rearwards which, again, entailed having the gun-trail split but, in this configuration, the cab top and sides could be left intact. The vehicle could be driven with the gun in either of the fighting positions but, for really going places, the 'touring trim' was used, with the gun out of action, facing forward over the cab and with the gun-trail unsplit. In this position, axle weights were 3 ton 6cwt 1qtr on the front and 4 ton 5cwt on the back, the gross, of course, remaining unchanged.

The 6-pounder was loaded and off-loaded using two hand-winches; it is just conceivable that one or two were built with power winches using the QLB chassis, hence the confusion in the official records, but the main production did not have powered winches, the work having to be done manually. The gunwheel and central trail ramps which were used when winching the gun aboard after changing positions from forward to rearward firing off – thankfully a task which did not have to be performed all that often – were carried in a locker beneath the body floor. At the rear, a steel superstructure supported a detachable canvas tilt inside which were four, demountable, tip-up crew seats. Ninety-six rounds of ammunition which were carried in lockers and gun shields were fitted to the sides of the body. The AT Portee was 19ft 3in in length and was 8ft 4½in wide. Its overall height was 10ft 2½in, but this could be reduced for shipping in the usual way by removing or, in this case, folding down, the cab top to give a height of 7ft 5½in without the gun or, with the gun loaded and facing rearwards – which was the lower option of the two – a height of 9ft.

Similar bodies were fitted to the Austin K5 and to the CMP

(Canadian Military Pattern) 3-tonners, the C60L and F60L models. After the war, most of the survivors of these types were converted to GS Cargo bodies, retaining their soft-top cabs.

Petrol tanks on the Anti-Tank Portee were standard, as fitted on all QLC chassis, being twin 16-gallon tanks mounted underneath the body. The reason for this was that the maximum deck-length was required, so placing the fuel tanks underneath, rather than behind the cab, as on the QLB, was a good idea. It also put them well away from the flash of firing guns, thus leading to a greater margin of safety for the crews.

Contract V4919 called for 1,126 AT Portees, numbers L4698419 to L4699544. The order was originally intended for QLC lorries '3 ton 4x4 (T)' – in other words for conversion to Troop Carrying Vehicles, (TCVs) – which would have cost £320.4.6d each. In April 1942, it was changed to Anti-Tank specification, on which the 6-pounder gun cost £90.11.9d. The fate of another contract, number V5121, which was amended in March 1942, may explain why things were changed. Dated February 1942, contract V5121 called for a total of 2,406 AT Portees on QLB chassis – although it now seems certain that they were built on QLC chassis. The contract, though, was substantially modified before its completion; the quantity was slashed to 388 vehicles (numbers L4916925 to L4917312) and the specification was changed: what were to have been AT Portees were changed to General Service Cargo bodies – but of a special kind. These had wooden bodies and open cabs, for use in the desert, and were delivered, by Brush Coachworks, between December 1942 and June 1943. The GS body cost £225 on top of the chassis/cab price of £312.19.7d, making a total of £537.19.7d.

A QLC Anti-Tank Portee, fully covered up with its tilt and thus indistinguishable, from the air and from general reconnaissance, from General Service lorries – to which most survivors were converted after the war. Note the position of the petrol tanks – indicative of the QLC chassis.

A victory parade shot showing the contribution which Bedford made to the war effort. By the end of the war Bedford had in fact supplied no less than 215,258 vehicles for the war effort. Note the ancient-looking civilian vehicles following the parade.

The Rations truck from B Echelon, the Wiltshire Regiment, in Krefeld in August 1949. The crossed keys insignia on the offside front wing represents 4 Inf Bde. From what can be seen of the census number – and the generally battered condition of the front end – this is quite an early model.

Cockatrice

Amongst the more unpleasant roles for which QLs were used was that of the mobile flame-thrower. Although this task was more commonly associated with tanks, mobile flame-throwers were actually developed on lorries, with the intention of using them for home defence. Two rival designs appeared on the scene in the early stages of development – one from Lagonda, the other from AEC. Lagonda's effort was built for the Petroleum Warfare Department, and used a sort of armoured van on a Commer chassis.

The AEC contender, which was known as the Heavy Pump Unit, was far more substantial, much of the design work being attributed to J G Rackham, who during the war served both as a tank designer and as an officer in the Tank Corps. He had worked for AEC before the war so, not surprisingly, his design was based upon an AEC chassis. The one chosen was the six-wheel-drive Model 0856 which was very similar in appearance to the Matador 4x4 heavy gun tractor and recovery vehicle, more properly known as the Model 0853. The eventual outcome of all this experimental work was the development of two production versions of the lorry-mounted flame-thrower under the codename Cockatrice. Six examples of the Heavy Cockatrice were built and allocated to the defence of RAF stations.

The regular Cockatrice was similar in design but smaller, being based on the QL chassis. WD contract V5039 called for 69 of these but, apparently – and for some unknown reason – only 60 went into service. Bodywork was supplied by Ratford Metal Bodies and they were specified as being "fitted for carriage of FUL equipment". The price, each, on the contract, which was dated October 12, 1943, was £405.18.9d for the vehicle, body and all its equipment. They were put into service around the country, having been issued for the protection of Royal Naval Air Stations. There appear to be no records of their performance in service – if, indeed, they were ever used – but, as one authority remarked, "Whilst they may not have been beautiful to look at, they looked stark and aggressive enough – and apparently worked quite well, at least on trial."

CHAPTER 5

QLC and other oddities

QLC was the version which was used for most applications which required a special body to be fitted, and this was usually done by some manufacturer other than Bedford. The QLC was supplied in chassis/cab form and was almost identical to the QLD except that it had twin petrol tanks and space for a larger body. The spare wheel was also different as it had to be stowed somewhere other than directly behind the cab, the usual place being at the back of the chassis.

The QLC chassis was thus used for such applications as tankers and fire tenders, troop carriers and, with house-type bodies, for mobile canteens, workshops, 'prophylactics' and a host of other roles including the QL articulated combination. It was also the chassis usually used for development and experimental work and

This RAF, 1,000-gallon tanker on a QLD chassis has been fitted with the diagonal wing strengtheners – visible just inboard of the sidelight – which appeared on all late models. The RAF operated several different types of tanker – for water, for fuel and lubricants and as aircraft refuellers, in which case they were fitted with booms and nozzles.

Rear view of the RAF tanker on a QLD chassis illustrated on the prevous page, showing the pumping equipment.

fulfilled certain very specialized roles like the 6-pounder Anti-Tank Portee and the Cockatrice. Altogether, about 7,000 QLCs were built. As well as the QLC, this chapter also looks at some of the other special bodies and special types supplied to the armed forces, produced on the QLD chassis.

Articulated combination

Bedford's QLC articulated tractor/trailer was designated 4x4-2, the military way of expressing the fact that a four-wheel-drive vehicle had a two-wheeled trailer attached to it. The load was carried in what, today, appears as an unusual way, with 1 ton in a small dropsided body on the tractor and 5 tons in the trailer. There were two reasons for this odd-looking arrangement. First was the fact that the standard 143in wheelbase chassis was used with relatively few modifications, apart from the artic coupling. This had to be placed above the rear axle, for load distribution reasons, which left a huge space between the back of the cab and the front of the semi-trailer. This not only looked wrong, but wasted an awful lot of vehicle so, to fill the gap, a small dropsided body of 1 ton capacity was mounted. Second was the fact that, with the load so far back, there would have been inadequate traction for the combination as a whole, so adding a ton at the front helped to keep the front wheels on the ground.

Although modifications to the standard chassis were relatively few, three are worth highlighting. First was the need to cut off the rear ends of the frame sidemembers; they served no useful purpose in the artic version and the steel could be used elsewhere – possibly even as the chassis extensions for the QLT! At the same time, additional crossmembers had to be fitted to carry the trailer coupling. Second, the brakes had to be modified to cope with 6-ton loads rather than 3-ton. The larger loads increased the gross laden weight of the combination to 10 ton 18cwt, compared with the standard QL's all-up weight of around 7 ton 10cwt. The modification required the fitment of a vacuum reservoir tank together with a vacuum gauge in the cab for the driver. Finally, and also to cope with the additional weight, the rear shock-absorbers were uprated.

Two manufacturers, Glover, Webb & Liversedge and the Scottish Motor Traction Co, were involved in building the trailers, although they were all built to the same design which was basically a General Service body with a flat floor – no wheel-boxes as on the rigid, QLD, version of the General Service truck – and a detachable canvas tilt and tubular steel bows.

The trailer was permanently coupled to the tractor by a 6 to 8-ton ball-coupling which was manufactured by Taskers of Andover. This allowed up to 20deg of movement either side and fore-and-aft and, it was felt, this made reasonable allowance for tilting on rough ground or for climbing or descending small hillocks.

The brakes on the trailer were operated, whilst on the move, in the conventional way, being linked into the vacuum-servo assisted footbrake system – hence the need for an additional vacuum reservoir. An additional brake was supplied to hold the vehicle when parked and this was in the form of a lever fitted to the trailer. It could only be applied from ground level and it was rather important to remember to release it before attempting to drive away. At its full gross weight and with the trailer handbrake on, 72bhp was simply not enough! Single rear tyres were retained, both on the tractor and the trailer, to improve cross-country performance – a slightly academic feature on the trailer as the wheels were not driven and any deviation from straight ahead would have nullified the advantage. It was, however, cheaper than twin rear wheels and much easier to maintain. A spare wheel for the trailer was carried in a retractable carriage above the trailer axle.

The recommended 'trailed weight' for the 4x4-2 on normal roads, was 6 tons, double the load rating for the standard QL. For hilly roads it was recommended that this was reduced to 4 tons and, for cross-country work, to 3 tons – giving little or no advantage over the plain, rigid, 3-ton capacity of the QLD. At 6 tons load – representing nearly 11 tons all-up – progress must have been rather leisurely, even on normal roads, as the same engine was used as in the rest of the Bedford range – including the MW 'pneumonia-wagons', which were only rated for 15cwt.

WD contract V4810, of April 25, 1942, called for 1,080 QLC 4x4-2s and production started on these soon thereafter. The batch was allocated numbers running from L558030 to L559109 but there is evidence of an earlier, prototype model which had the number L555423.

Chapter 4 showed that anomalies arose with Census Number prefixes and the QLC artic was one of those anomalies. Most articulated tractor, or motive, units are capable of being matched to several different types of trailer. In other words, they are interchangeable and the trailers are detachable. In such cases the unit was considered as a tractor and it was given an 'H' prefix. If the trailer was *not* detachable, the tractor unit and its trailer was allocated an 'L' prefix. An example of the detachable trailer combination is the Bedford OY 4x2-2, which was fitted with Scammell automatic coupling, much favoured in civilian life by the railway companies, on their little 'mechanical horses'; the tractor was capable of independent operation so had an 'H' prefix.

Two of the contracts placed for articulated combinations are of interest in this context. Contract S2410 specifies simply *tractors* – no quantity is defined but the number H5204997 (and probably onwards from that number) is allocated. Another contract, dated May 1943, *does* specify a quantity – one, but it is for a QLD, not a QLC. This calls for a conversion to a tractor unit, suggesting that it, too, could have been a prototype, but possibly for a different specification. Weight is added to this conjecture by the 'H' prefix. It seems likely, therefore, that these two contracts may both have been for a prototype artic tractor *with a detachable trailer*, one on a QLC chassis and one on a QLD, probably fitted with Scammell automatic coupling gear. Retention of the 143in wheelbase, together with the unusually high ground clearance of the QL, probably rendered a solution involving a detachable trailer impossible at economic cost.

S T C Bryan, formerly of 490 GT Coy RASC, recalls that during 1943, QLC artics were shipped to North Africa where they were used to service the docks at Phillipville taking stores and supplies inland to Constantine. This is a very hilly area and the trucks were worked hard and long – to the extent that two weaknesses became apparent: firstly, constant use on wide throttle openings, laden and uphill in low gears, caused the exhaust valves to burn out; secondly, probably also attributable to the particularly strenuous work they were being called upon to perform, the trailer had a habit of overturning.

L558777 is one of a batch of over 1,000 of these QLC 6-ton semi-trailer outfits built in 1942. These came to be called, in some circles, 'dromedaries' because of their two humps, load being carried in the main semi-trailer as well as in the dog-box on the tractor chassis. These artics did not qualify for an 'H' prefix because, in the normal run of events, the trailer could not be uncoupled.

A 4x4-2 articulated combination, built on the QLC chassis. This one dates from 1942 and is one of a batch of 1,080 vehicles, the bodies for which were supplied by Glover, Webb & Liversedge and Scottish Motor Traction. The photo shows women at work painting on the 'Mickey Mouse' camouflage, assisted by youths underage for call-up.

A remedy for the burnt-out exhaust valves was soon found as the ever-resourceful Tommies did not take long to come up with the idea of using valves from tank engines – a cure which apparently worked! (Churchill tanks had Bedford engines.)

The second problem took rather more solving. As already mentioned, the trailer was permanently attached to the unit, not by a kingpin as on modern-day artics, nor even by the Scammell gear, but by a very simple ball-joint. The lugs which carried the retaining bolts for this coupling tended to suffer metal fatigue and would, reportedly, 'often' break, resulting in a trailer overturn. This seems hardly surprising given that the allowable tilt on the coupling, side-to-side and fore-and-aft, was only 20deg, which is quite satisfactory for most road conditions which are likely to be encountered, but a little on the 'thin' side for anything which involved rough ground. How often these supporting lugs gave way is not recorded; neither is the fact that a trailer overturn may have caused the lugs to break, rather than vice versa!

So hard-worked were these vehicles in North Africa that many finished their lives as scrap at the Return Vehicle Depot at Bizerta, whilst others were taken over by Italian prisoners-of-war when the British forces returned to the UK. None seems to have survived into preservation.

The technical specification of the QLC Artic, apart from the differences mentioned, was the same as for the general specification except, of course, that it had very different dimensions. The length of the tractor and semi-trailer together was 30ft 6in; it was 7ft 6in wide and 10ft 8in high. The semi-trailer alone measured, overall, 17ft 8in in length and, inside the body it was 16ft 11in long and 6ft 10in wide. The body sides were 1ft 6in high and the loading height, under the tilt, was exactly 6ft. The loading height at the rear, in the unladen state was 4ft 6in. Various parts could be removed, as with the other models, to give a stripped shipping height of 7ft 6in.

Tankers

The armed forces used large numbers of tankers for various purposes including petrol, aviation spirit, lubricants and water. Most of them were supplied on 4x2 chassis which, from Bedford, centred around the MW, OX and OY models although some were supplied (or converted) on the OL (not QL) chassis, which was of the conventional, civilian appearance of the immediate prewar Bedford 3 to 4 tonners with twin rear wheels. Those supplied on QL chassis, whilst basically similar, were of many different specifications.

Those supplied to the RAF, who were major users, were of several basic types: contract V4481, placed in January 1942, called for *1,000*-gallon fuel tankers and contract V5160, of July 1945, called for *950*-gallon tanks to be supplied – by Butterfields of Shipley, Yorkshire. This serves to illustrate the two basic types of tank, supplied both to the Army and to the RAF, early models being 1,000-gallon, later ones, 950-gallon.

The 1,000-gallon tankers were supplied complete with 'pto' (power take-off) for driving on-board pumps. The pto was taken from a point on the transfer gearbox case and was operated by a remote engine throttle control: the pto was a feature of several different QL roles, including the QLB, the QLR and the winch-tipper QLW.

The 950-gallon version had two rear and two side lockers. The rear lockers housed a total of eight lengths of hose; six for fuel delivery, being 10ft 3in long and of 1½in bore, and two for suction, being 11ft 11in long and of 2in bore. The side compartments housed, on the nearside, a small petrol engine – either a 3hp Bradford or a P5XC Stuart-Turner – which drove, via worm reduction gears, two drum pumps for fuel delivery. Usually the pumps were manufactured by Zwicky Ltd, of Slough. The side compartments also carried an air-separator, pumping control valves, two flow-meters and a suction filter. Fuel delivery capacity was 30 to 40 gallons per minute through one boom and nozzle or 55 to 65 through two.

It was a requirement for fuel tankers that chassis had to be fitted with a full-depth guard behind the cab to ensure that no sparks or 'stray heat' came into contact with fuel vapours. This meant that the window shutter in the rear of the cab had to be blanked off and the exhaust system also had to be re-routed, exhausting just beneath the radiator. This re-routing of the exhaust pipe required some of the frontal appendages on the cab to be fitted the reverse way round, particularly noticeable being the starting handle which was mounted to the left instead of the right. Some tankers, such as the Bedford OYC, were fitted with attachments to accept tilt-bows, for with a tilt over the top of the tank, there was nothing to suggest to aerial reconnaissance that the vehicle was a tanker – and thus a

These two QLD fire tenders are both from the first production batch of 299 vehicles, 14 of which were specially prepared for duties in the Arctic. The bodies were built by Austin and the last ones were put into service in the summer of 1943. Note the non-standard tilt-bows and the hooks for the ladder. In service, these tenders towed a small trailer which, for shipping, could be loaded into the body.

prime target. No evidence can be found to suggest that this was ever done with the QL.

A variation on the standard fuel tanker was the aircraft refuelling tankers, for the RAF. These were fitted with either two or three booms mounted on a platform at the front end of the carrier tank, for over-wing filling. Each boom had 12ft of hose and terminated in a trigger-type filling nozzle. The outer two booms were connected to the fuel system and the centre one to the oil system, the booms themselves being 13ft long and described as 'self-elevating'. This is something of an understatement as the springs which 'assisted' the self-elevation were extremely powerful and quite capable of lifting a man from the ground unless carefully controlled, as discovered by the author when working on 19AD40 in 1985 – the year in which the vehicle was found, in a barn – by which time the springs were over 40 years old!

The three-boom version had a two-compartment tank, divided to hold, at the front end, 100 gallons of lubricating oil and, in the rear compartment, 850 gallons of fuel. When the vehicle was in use for refuelling, or defuelling, turbo-prop aircraft with AVTUR – after the war – the lube-oil compartment and its associated boom was not used.

On occasion, tankers were used with a trailer. These were usually manufactured by Brockhouse and, when towed behind QLs, used the standard towing hitch on its leaf spring. These Brockhouse-produced trailers were examples of what was known as the Bellamy type, having a four-wheeled chassis and a tank of 900 gallons capacity. They had a triangular, or A-frame, drawbar and a swivelling towing-eye and were usually equipped with a Lister 42QA petrol engine driving Zwicky pumps. Another, different specification of Brockhouse trailer was also available – the Brockhouse Mark II – which had a capacity of 5 tons, but there is no evidence of these having been towed by QLs.

Fuel consumption of the standard rig was estimated at 7mpg – compared with 8mpg for the standard cargo versions – or as 5mpg for 'camp-running' which, inevitably, involved mostly low-gear work and, on some versions, use of the power take-off (pto).

Tankers on airfield duties logged very low mileages (19AD40, the airfield refueller referred to earlier, had 1,200 miles on the clock in 1985 and was in a condition which suggested that this was a genuine reading!). As a result, some of them were very long-lived and many were reworked just after the war and in the early Fifties, again, mainly for the RAF. After the war, those still in service with the RAF were allocated Stores Reference Numbers, as follows:

Reference	Description
16A/700	850gall gas/100gall oil tank – with booms
16A/1297	850gall AVTUR refueller – with booms
16A/1393	950gall refueller with booms and pto drive
16A/699	850gall petrol/100gall oil – without booms

Water tankers differed in a number of respects. Both filling and emptying was by gravity, filling being through a top manhole with a domed cover, and emptying being through 2in valves, one fitted either side.

Many tankers which survived service life had a second lease of life as civilian bowsers of one sort or another and several have survived into preservation including some 950-gallon airfield refuellers and a variety of Army, RAF and 'unclassified' petrol tankers and water bowsers.

Fire tenders

Fire tenders were supplied mainly for guarding airfields and for the protection of fuel and ammunition dumps and, as such, had two distinct functions: the rendering of first aid for smaller fires and, for more extensive conflagrations, serious fire-fighting.

Built on the QLD chassis, the basic body of the vehicle was externally similar to the metal-bodied General Service lorry with tilt, except that the body was slightly longer making the vehicle 20ft 2in overall compared with the usual 19ft 8in of the QLD GS. Its normal height was 10ft 1in but this could be reduced, for shipping, to exactly 7ft. The body also had four lockers cut into the front part and a shallower tail-gate flap, to permit rapid access. Its main equipment consisted of a 200-gallon water tank mounted centrally in the forward end of the body together with a first-aid hose reel mounted between the body and the cab; there was also a pump which was driven from the pto and, as with the tankers, hand-controlled by a remote engine throttle. This equipment, which fulfilled the first-aid role of the outfit, could be put into action instantly on arrival at a fire.

For fires which required rather more than first aid, a trailer pump was towed, usually with either a Coventry Climax or a Godiva pump. Fixtures were provided on the vehicle to carry a hook ladder as well as a 30ft extension ladder which was hung from the tilt superstructure and which protruded both fore and aft. Side-lockers were provided in which to carry the suction hose and all the necessary nozzles for the trailer pump, together with various types of fire extinguisher. For shipping purposes the trailer could be stowed in the body of the vehicle.

Finally, to make it quite distinctive, it carried a warning bell – compulsory equipment for all fire-fighting equipment! – and a large red board proclaiming ARMY FIRE SERVICE across the top of the windscreen. A giveaway for identifying fire tenders which may, later, have been converted to other roles, is the rear wheelarch which is cut out in 'three-penny bit' style, rather than the rectangular shape of the conventional wheelarch.

The prototype Fire Tender was ordered on WD contract S2941, dated April 1943. It was delivered on June 7, 1943, having been allocated Census Number L5204998. The chassis/cab cost £347.6.8d and the body which, on this prototype, was built by Brush Engineering Ltd, and for which a separate contract was placed, cost

£535.0.0d. Several other contracts followed, the first being later in June 1943, for another 299 complete vehicles (with Census Numbers L5294819 to L5295117), the building of the special fire-tender bodies being sub-contracted out to the Austin Motor Company. By November 1943, a further contract had been placed for yet another 150 vehicles (L5458288 to L5458437) so, clearly, the specification was fulfilling the requirements set for it. Finally, in July 1944, a contract was placed for no less than 553 chassis of which 290 (numbers L5863231 to L5863520) had bodies built by Eccles; the remainder (L5863521 to L5863783), which were to have been built by Austin, were cancelled.

With an all-up weight of only 6 ton 14cwt 3qtr, the Fire Tender was a little livelier than some of its more heavily burdened brethren. Fully loaded, its weight was distributed with, on the front axle, 2 ton 15cwt and, on the rear axle, 3 ton 19cwt 3qtr.

Miscellaneous types
Under this heading fall any number of special applications of the QL chassis/cab although not a single one is listed in the *Data Book of Wheeled Vehicles – Army Transport, 1939-1945*. However, research in various museum archives has revealed the some-time existence of a number of interesting types.

House-type bodies
House-type, or box, bodies were fitted on QLC chassis for at least two types: the 'QLC Studio W/T' and the 'QLC TEV Corps Type C'. Both of these are very similar to bodies which were predominantly fitted on QLR chassis and are dealt with in Chapter 7. Surviving records also show other house-type bodies as having been fitted, but the quality of the clerical records is not consistent and some of the

Interior of a Field Kitchen clearly showing its QLD derivation. Large numbers of these were built on QL chassis and they were often a very welcome sight to hungry and battle-weary troops.

A QLC mobile dental laboratory, very similar in general appearance to the mobile clinic or 'prophylactic' body which did not, usually, tow a trailer. For some reason, this rig is on non-standard Firestone 'Ground-Grip' tyres rather than the conventional Dunlop 'Trak-Grip'.

special types listed as QLD (General Service – Cargo) chassis conversions may not, in fact, have been conversions at all, being built straight onto a QLC chassis/cab. Amongst these are:

Mobile kitchens

The first reference to mobile kitchens appears on contract V5159, which was for 2,000 QLDs, but which was 'interfered with' by extracting one of them (L4912911) to be prototyped as a Field, or Mobile, Kitchen. Car Cruiser Caravans made the conversion and later picked up significant numbers of orders for the production version at a price of £92.11.2d each.

A contract for 200 mobile kitchens was then placed by the War Department, in 1943, and these were issued with Census Numbers L5366021 to L5366220. Another contract, also dated 1943, called for no less than 1,260 mobile kitchens but these are listed as being on QLD *and* on QLR chassis. It is evident that some were, indeed, built on QLD chassis, but because the QLR chassis embodied a number of specific, technical modifications to allow it to carry radio equipment without interference from the engine, it seems very unlikely that such an expensive chassis would be 'wasted' on kitchens.

On another contract for mobile kitchens, Car Cruiser Caravans supplied 473 bodies and T Harrington & Co supplied a further 370. Much is made of the type of bins to be provided under this contract – which was mixed with a requirement for some TEV bodies for W/T vehicles. The body-builders had the choice of providing either 'four bins S-type, four bins Y-type' at £22 per set or 'two bins S-type, two bins Z-type' at £11 per set, 'six bins Y-type, two bins Z-type' (unpriced!) or simply two bins S-type. Frustratingly, no information is given, or can be found, concerning the differences between these types or their precise function.

Mobile canteen, dental laboratory, etc

Very similar to the mobile kitchen in general appearance was the mobile canteen, sometimes designated Type 145, the nearside of

which was fitted with a serving hatch. The earliest reference to this type appears in 1943 where L5303128, a Type J145 House Type, is recorded, with chassis number 29474, although it is unclear whether this eventually became a canteen or a dental laboratory. The contract for the batch which included L5303128 was S3538, work on which was suspended resulting in the cancellation of 650 vehicles to give priority to fire tenders and QLRs. A total of 209 QLC GS was also called for on this contract, amongst which would have been the 'House Type' conversions, by Alexanders (for 200), SMT (for five vehicles) and Spurlings (for a further four). It is these which probably suffered the cancellation as the remainder of the contract was for QLTs and QLRs for which demand was still strong.

Dental laboratories, mobile dental clinics or 'prophylactics', as they and some other clinics were sometimes called, were operated by the RADC and were equipped with all the paraphernalia required to operate in the field. This included the inevitable dentist's chair, plus all the necessary medication and instrument lockers as well as large water tanks. The interior, which was painted a pale *eau-de-nil* colour, was lit by electric roof-lamps assisted by three windows, high up in each side of the vehicle, and entry – and escape! – was through a narrow door at the rear.

Generator lorry supplied to the RAF as an alternative to the trailer-mounted generator. This version featured a special, flat deck without the wheelboxes of the normal QLD on which it is based. A raised platform was then built inside on which to install a generator.

Accumulator-charging workshop

Accumulator-charging workshops are one example of the many container-style bodies which the RAF used, all of which were basically similar, but with subtle differences depending upon their exact role. The accumulator-charging workshop, or battery-charging container, had a welded steel frame with hardboard panelling and was fitted with a sheet metal floor. Sliding windows, complete with blackout shutters, were cut in the sides and in the front and rear bulkheads. The access door was at the rear, reached by steps which could be stowed in the body. Each side of the body had three battery charging units with slotted wooden boards on which to stand accumulators; cupboards were fitted underneath. Located against the front bulkhead were two Type 7C rectifying units and an accumulator capacity testing set, together with Winchesters for distilled water and a carrier for acid containers. Externally, along each side, was a slotted iron platform, 10ft in length, which gave additional standing space for accumulators on charge. The whole unit could be serviced by an independent 230-volt power supply from an external source – occasionally an enclosed trailer with a mobile generating set.

SPECIAL TYPES

Giraffe

As early as 1942 detailed plans were being made for a seaborne invasion of the continental mainland and it was realized, from experiences in the Mediterranean, that a method of waterproofing vehicles was required so that they could be unloaded quickly by driving them off landing craft which had been beached. Experiments were carried out by several manufacturers with various ways and means of enabling vehicles to pass through relatively deep water without 'drowning' the electrical system or 'inhaling' water into the carburettor. As an alternative approach experiments were made in which all the mechanical parts which could be affected by sea water were placed high enough to clear all but the deepest water. The result, from Bedford's engineers, was a strange looking vehicle with its cab and engine raised, by about 4ft, on struts.

Access to the cab for the driver and passenger must have been a

A Merryweather cable-operated fire escape mounted on a QLC chassis. It is quite possible that this is the trial prototype for what went into production as the Simon Observation Post towers but, equally, could have been a QL-based experiment with fire escapes which, in the event, were mounted on DUKWs for the Normandy invasion.

difficult process – even the normal version requires quite a climb! Drive from the engine and gearbox was taken, by chains, to the main transfer box mounted in its usual position. Once ashore the vehicle would have made a superb target as it towered high above anything around it and would have been highly conspicuous. Fortunately, methods of waterproofing were improved in order to be capable of local application, so this was another of those development jobs which failed to make it.

The waterproofing method eventually adopted consisted of covering all the vulnerable parts with a special compound which came to be known as WD Plastic Putty. Whilst this took an inordinate amount of time to carry out – up to 55 man-hours for some vehicle types – it had the advantage of being cheap and relatively simple to perform. Vauxhall, themselves, trained REME fitters who, in turn, trained unit personnel in the 'art' of waterproofing.

Bedford Bren

With the threatened drying-up of supplies of rubber after the capture of Singapore, and in a general attempt to save raw materials, the Ministry of Supply carried out an experiment in which a Bren-gun carrier's running-gear was mated to a standard QL Cargo lorry. Surviving photographs indicate that, as with the Giraffe, a QLD chassis was used but it was, nevertheless, most certainly a 'special type'. The track and suspension assembly from the Bren carrier was modified, mainly by shortening it, and exhaustive tests were carried out at the WVEE.

This hybrid QL performed even better than had been hoped, and certainly better than existing half-tracks because, unlike the earlier marques, the QL had a driven front axle. Several reasons combined to prevent the design going into full production: its initial cost was obviously higher than two simple wheels; it was far more complex than an axle with wheels and, of course, huge strides had been made in developing synthetic substitutes for rubber which, effectively, removed the reason for developing the idea in the first place. The prototype was either reconverted to a standard lorry or scrapped as there is no evidence that it survived or was ever used.

Observation towers

During 1944 a need was identified for mobile observation towers and, needless to say, the choice of chassis was the QL. For a description of the product which was eventually produced, one cannot do better than to refer to the official document, *SIMON OBSERVATION TOWER (Model 25S/QLD) – Description and Instructions for Operation* issued by ADOS (Local Resources), ORD 6, on May 4, 1945:

"This observation tower is designed to be extremely mobile, quick to operate and gives a point of view approximately 85ft (at maximum height) above ground level.

"It is constructed on the Bedford Chassis, QLD Type, for mobility

The Bedford Bren, another, very costly, prototype which had many useful features. However, its main purpose was to save rubber, and with the development of synthetics this, too, never progressed beyond the prototype stage.

and can be raised to full height in two minutes. The lowering of the tower takes less than one minute and, if necessary, the vehicle can move during this operation.

"Briefly, the tower consists of three sets of telescopic tubes, which are made of special steel, very accurately machined and being very strong in relation to their weight. The three sets are fixed together to form a triangular section for rigidity.

"The tower is carried in a horizontal position and is hinged near its centre of gravity to a sub-chassis or frame which is provided with quick-action screws for levelling the whole assembly. A pendulum sight determines the level point and the complete levelling operation can be done in a few seconds.

"The operation of raising the tower, in both stages, from horizontal to vertical, and the extension, is done hydraulically. A gear pump, driven from the power take-off on the transfer box, pumps oil into a cylinder and the piston movement provides the force to push the tower into an upright position. Oil is then directed by a hand-operated valve to the base of each set of tubes which rapidly extend.

"Safety devices are included in the design to prevent any collapse of the tower if any part of the mechanism is accidentally damaged, and to enable the tower to remain at any required height indefinitely without any need for running the engine.

"To increase the stability, extending legs are provided with adjustable feet so that the track is greatly increased and the spring action of the chassis is 'ironed-out'. If greater stability is required for instruments to be used on the platform, guy ropes may be attached to the loops provided on the top two sections."

The towers actually consisted of five sections topped by a circular platform and, when swung forward to the transport position, they rested in a bracket fitted to the top of a large hydraulic oil tank

69

behind the cab. This feature would have entailed resiting the spare wheel to make room for the hydraulic oil tank, the most likely location being beneath the tailboard, as on the QLT. A ladder was provided for the observer to reach the platform once the tower was erected, but not elevated.

It appears that at least 10 of these towers were produced and it is known that the Canadians fitted the same equipment on the Diamond T, Model 975, 6x6 chassis, but these could have been the originals refitted to a more suitable and stable vehicle. Coincidentally, whilst researching these towers, the author was asked to help identify just such equipment which had turned up in Dorset fitted on a Bedford RL chassis – the RL being the successor to the QL, introduced in the early Fifties. It is not known whether any saw active service.

Folding boat equipment, experimental pontoon, etc
The Royal Engineers used numbers of QLs of various types, but mainly QLD GS, in active service, for carrying such materials (or 'materiel' as the military prefer to spell it) as bridge parts, sandbags, explosives, barbed wire and all the other paraphernalia required in their line of business.

At home, under the aegis of the RE, fell various experimental establishments which were quite separate from the MWEE (Mechanised Warfare Experimental Establishment) and the WVEE (Wheeled Vehicle Experimental Establishment). Before the war an Experimental Bridging Establishment had been set up at Christchurch, Hampshire and an Experimental Demolition Establishment at Bovington, Dorset. These fell under the control of the Ministry of Supply whilst the remaining parts of the Royal Engineers and Signals Board – formerly all one organization – remained with the DREE (Directorate of Royal Engineer Equipment).

It was to this establishment that two QLC chassis/cabs were issued, under contract S2796, for conversion to, as the official military nomenclature described them, 'Tractor, 4x4-2 FBE Bedford/Tasker' and 'Tractor 4x4-2 Pontoon Bedford/Tasker'. The FBE stood for 'Folding Boat Equipment' and, whilst every source investigated mentions both of these, there seem to be no details surviving, and little can be gleaned from photographs. It is known that they were both given a Chilwell Reference, number 174 for the experimental pontoon and 175 for the FBE. They were also allocated numbers with an 'H' prefix, rather than the 'L' which was the standard for Bedford 4x4-2s, but the numbers were issued in the reverse sequence to the Chilwell numbers. Thus the FBE was H5469698 and the Pontoon was H5469699. The contract for these two was placed with Bedford on March 29, 1943, calling for delivery "not later than the first week in April" so, clearly, these had to be abstracted from the routine production on some other contract.

The price for the FBE and the Pontoon was £344.7.9d each for the chassis/cab and Tasker charged a mere £24.10.2d for their part of the work. Total cost as supplied to the military was thus £368.17.11d but the costs incurred by the RE, in constructing the actual equipment, is not known. One can only surmise that the experiments were not successful, at least with the QL, as nothing ever went into production.

Another curiosity, about which little is known, is the single vehicle ordered on V4393 and assigned to the Experimental Tunnelling Establishment (ETE) which was, as its name suggests, charged with research into mechanical tunnelling. Amongst its other duties was research into better ways of digging trenches. As has so often been the case throughout history, generals and politicians are always preparing to fight 'the last war' – in this case the 1914-18 war – so envisaged a large role for trenches and hence mechanical equipment for digging them.

Volume VIII of the *History of the Corps of Royal Engineers,* which covers the period 1938-48, notes that the ETE grew out of the Special Tunnelling Training and Development Centre which had been set up at the SME at Ripon in 1941. Headed by Lt Col C D A Fenwick, it moved to Christchurch in 1942 on completion of its training role, where it came under the same control as the other 'ExEs' (Experimental Establishments).

Retaining a separate identity from the Bridging ExE, its role was to develop mining techniques and equipment, including ancillary electrical and mechanical plant and the use of explosives. In 1946 the ETE together with other related units were merged to become MEXE (the Military Engineering ExE) which developed the present day Mexefloat used in the Falklands conflict.

The single vehicle, a QLD GS, was given Chilwell Reference 192 and WD number L5306777. Delivered in September 1943, the only positive information traceable about it is that it was on smaller wheels and different tyres from the standard version – 10.50 x 16in instead of the usual 10.50 x 20in – and that its price, ex works, was £421.4.7d.

CHAPTER 6

QLD, QLT and QLW

This chapter assesses the three models of the QL which, together, accounted for the majority of their production. The QLD – the 'bulk standard' General Service lorry – was used by just about every part of the armed forces which had an off-road load carrying requirement. It was also used as the basis for many of the more straightforward conversions – to such objects as mobile kitchens and fire tenders, for example. The QLT was the famous long-bodied 'Trooper', based on the QLC chassis with bodies produced and fitted by a variety of makers, of which Austin was the most common. The QLW came into service towards the end of the war as an air-portable tipper equipped with a winch, this giving the clue to its being built upon the QLB chassis.

So, for what outwardly look like three very similar vehicles, there are three different chassis types: QLB for the QLW, QLC for the QLT and plain QLD. Small wonder that the official records sometimes became confused!

QLD
The QLD was the Army's most numerous off-road 3-ton General Service load carrier. Apart from the QLC which was supplied in chassis/cab form, the 'D' was the basic QL vehicle. It had a metal body with a wooden floor into which were cut trap-doors to give access to, and facilitate maintenance of, chassis components. Into the tops of the sides were set recesses to accept the tilt-bows, or hoops, over which the canvas body was hung. Tilts were usually a simple rectangle of canvas which was lashed down along the sides with large flaps to fold in at the front and rear, although some tailored versions could also be seen, especially after the war, when some of them had been 're-canvassed'. The tailboard, which lowered right down for loading, had D-shaped holes cut into the nearside and offside panels to act as a step for access. An intermediate

A very famous photograph taken in the North African desert, and reproduced by permission of Vauxhall Motors, showing yet another QLD being used in a troop carrying role.

position was available, in which chains held the tailboard horizontal to act as an extension to the load platform.

The QLD's overall height was exactly 10ft, but this could be reduced, for shipping, to 8ft 6in even with the tilt in position. This was done by unshipping the tilt bows and placing them on the load-deck. Ground clearance, under the differentials, was a full 1ft. Inside the body, the length was 12ft 5in, the width 7ft 5in and the height exactly 6ft. Unladen, the QLD, in its GS version, weighed 3 ton 4cwt 2qtr; laden, it tipped the scales at 6 ton 17cwt 2qtr.

The QLD was occasionally used as a troop carrier, with lower capacity than the QLT and, when used in this role, a knotted rope was suspended from the centre of the rear tilt-bow, a highly characteristic feature in common with the QLT, further to assist access.

M F Reid, of St Albans, formerly with the Wiltshire Regiment in Krefeld, considers he was "privileged" to drive a QLD Troop Carrier which was, he says, "...the sweetest vehicle I have ever driven". He recalls that the high cab and flat front gave exceptional all-round vision which was particularly useful when driving "on the wrong side of the road" in Germany.

Also remembered is the welcome warmth, in winter, from having the engine in the cab. If more heat was wanted, it was common practice to open the inspection trap in the engine cover, so that waves of hot air – and noise – surrounded the occupants. Those who served in the desert with QLs might have found the heat rather less

73

welcome, but one could always open the windscreens, the machine-gun hatch, both windows and the sliding metal panel in the rear bulkhead of the cab – and even then, it could still get fairly hot!

After the war, many of the surviving QLDs were sold into civilian work where they were snapped up and, almost literally, worked to death. When new, they offered an amazing – by 1945 standards – 10bhp or so per ton, laden, with colossal tractive effort (1,490lb per ton) so quite large numbers found work in vehicle recovery and timber extraction. Many have survived and, amongst these, there is often to be found quite a large element of re-build and cannibalization. However, even if not totally 'original', they are a wonderfully evocative sight – and sound.

The first contract ever placed for QLs was, as has been seen, V3949, for 4,272 vehicles of which 2,501 were QLDs. The basic cost price was £411.4.0d and the contract was placed on February 8, 1940; some records suggest later dates – right up to July 1942 – but February 8 appears on the most reliable of the surviving records. The later dates probably refer to amendments which, progressively, increased the number of 'D's on this contract to a total of 3,233.

However, associated with contract V3949 was another contract for QL General Service (GS) lorries, and details from the two documents overlap. The contract in question was V4090, placed on August 2, 1940, for 715 vehicles; later one was added, for conversion to a W/T truck for the RAOC (L4671779). Of the original 715, 42 were delivered to the RASC depot at Slough whilst the other 673 were delivered to Chilwell for allocation to other units. This latter

An oddity about which nothing appears in the official records, this QLD has been converted to run on 'producer-gas' made by burning charcoal whilst on the move. The idea was tried out mostly in civilian operations, especially for buses, but was abandoned as soon as practicable as performance was severely curtailed.

batch was cancelled at one stage after having had WD numbers allocated to it (from L4532267 to L4532939), but these vehicles were reinstated and allocated numbers which were interspersed with those in contract V3949. This reflects the old procedure whereby Census Numbers were allocated upon receipt of the vehicle into service – or at least into the Army's possession; later they were allocated at the contract stage and applied during painting, hence some numbers not being taken up when the contracts were cancelled.

Many other contracts were placed for GS Cargo lorries, including some which required 'outside' suppliers to fit GS bodies on to QLC chassis/cabs. Others had subtle peculiarities written into the contract for some special item or other. One such called for a total of 2,000 vehicles, 252 of which were to be 'converted to Fuel & Water'. Unfortunately, no details of what this conversion involved have survived.

Other peculiarities on the same contract include the fitting of one vehicle (L5242132) with mine-detector equipment in a swivel-mounted rear drum. Another was supplied to the BBC and was used in the transmission of live broadcasts from the field during and after the D-Day Normandy invasion. Two others from this contract were supplied to the WVEE but, again, there is no record as to the purpose for which they were used. The vehicles on this contract were numbered L5241501 to L5243500 and were supplied at an ex-works price of £411.17.5d.

Reference is made elsewhere in this book to a mixed batch of 2,000 QLC GS, QLTs and QLRs. This particular contract was curtailed to give priority to QLRs and fire tenders for which an urgent need had arisen. The final number delivered was 1,350 vehicles, of which 209 were GS Cargo, 26 were QLR and 1,115 were for troop carrying. The GS bodies were fitted onto the QLC chassis by outside suppliers, before delivery – ostensibly as QLDs. There may also have been some house-types on this contract with mobile canteen, dental laboratory and similar bodies, most of which were supplied by Alexanders, SMT and Spurlings.

Some of the troop-carrying bodies, also supplied by third party contractors, usually Austin, may have been converted to QLT specification by the addition of a chassis extension for example, and some may have been supplied as if they were QLDs in Troop Carrying Vehicle (TCV) style, having a lower passenger capacity than the QLT, with fewer seats because the body was shorter. Carbodies Ltd supplied 450 bodies at a price of £161.15.0d and 665 were supplied by Normand, at £240.10.0d, which suggests that the Normand bodies were made to the full QLT specification. By comparison, the QLR bodies built by Dennis Bros on this contract cost £401.12.0d. The WD numbers allocated to the contract as a whole were L5303008 to L5305007, but only those up to L5304357 were taken up.

Oddly, although full price detail is specified for the TCV and other body types in the contract, no prices are quoted for those built to GS specification by Alexanders, SMT and Spurlings, other than for the chassis cab from Bedford, which cost £346.9.10d. Deliveries commenced in October 1943 rising to 290 per month by March 1944. Although all deliveries against this contract should have been complete, according to the schedule, well before February 1945, there is a contract rider which states that any remaining to be delivered after February 23, 1945, had to be made suitable for operation in the tropics.

As already mentioned, QLDs were sometimes converted to other types including tankers, fire tenders, field kitchens and the like. Other specials include one which was sent to be fully waterproofed. This one, which could well have been for the Giraffe mentioned in Chapter 5, was an addition to the original order, was then cancelled and later reinstated, each time leaving a – slightly indistinct – trail of contract numbers, cancellation references and general confusion!

In October 1944 a contract for 4,000 'D's was placed, priced at £444 ex works. The whole batch was APT *and* '...suitable for use in the tropics'. Numbered L6124332 to L6128331, at least two of this batch have survived into preservation. One, L6125084, released from service as 47YW62, chassis number 48097, is kept at Horley, Surrey, and the other, L6125561, latterly 43YW60, chassis number 48998,

What at first appears to be a conventional QLD turns out to be another 'special', this time in the form of a special steel body, known as the 'US Type Steel', which has no wheelboxes, thus presenting a flat floor, albeit with an even higher tailboard than the usual version. This vehicle was probably one of about 10 special-bodied versions produced by SMT and Spurlings on a contract for 2,000 assorted vehicles.

was the author's proud possession. This batch was scheduled for delivery from June 1945 at the rate of 590 per month so would have missed the D-Day landings by a full year. L6125561, however, served with 15 Field Park Company[1] in support of 17, 245 and 253 Field Companies[2], RE as part of 3 Inf Div which did *not* miss D-Day! This unit landed in R (Roger) sector, the westernmost point on Sword Beach, between the port of Ouistreham and Lion sur Mer. One of the first tasks assigned to them was to build two Class 40 tidal pontoon bridges, one over the River Orne, at Benouville, and the other – now known as Pegasus Bridge – over the Caen canal at Ranville if the existing bridges were not captured intact. They were then engaged in the capture of Caen. The QL's task in all this was to carry engineers' supplies to the sappers involved in these tasks. With the surrender at Luneburg Heath having taken place before L6125561 rolled off the production lines it is unlikely that she saw very much European service; she did, however, see service in Cyprus many years later.

It has already been seen that the first contract placed for QLs was for GS Cargo lorries, type QLD: so, indeed, was the last. This was S9548, dated May 23, 1945, for 2,000 vehicles having both the tropicalized and the APT specification. The contract was marked BREAK CLAUSE and, in fact, was reduced to 392 vehicles with WD numbers L6272781 to L6273172. Numbers up to L6274780 were allocated to the original full quantity.

Footnotes
1. The Arm of Service sign for 15 Field Park Company was the number 49 in white numerals on a pale blue background. The sign for 3 Inf Div was a red disc with three equilateral triangles, arranged in an equilateral triangle, apex upwards.

2. World War Two nomenclature refers to Field Companies (and Field Park Companies in support). After the war the term was changed to Squadron.

QLT
The QLT Troop Carrying Vehicle, (TCV), usually known as the 'Trooper', differed in appearance from the QLD in that it had an extended chassis and body. It also had an extended exhaust pipe to cater for the longer body, and to carry exhaust fumes to the rear, well away from the passengers – a feature which could usefully have been adopted on the QLD TCV as, with the tilt closed up, one could almost choke in the back of the 'D' version! The Trooper also had the twin 16-gallon petrol tanks of the QLC upon which it was based, and the spare wheel was carried in a cradle under the rear of the chassis as on the QLC.

Instead of a conventional tailboard, some QLTs – those with all-metal bodies built, predominantly, by Austin but also by Marshalls of Cambridge[1] – were fitted with rear doors which, with the aid of a

Footnote
1. Marshalls of Cambridge now own the manufacturing and design rights of what was the Bedford trucks business.

step attached to the rear of the chassis, enabled passengers simultaneously to board on both the left and the right-hand side. However, some bodies were put out to other contracts, and some of these can be identified by having wooden bodies and conventional tailboards. As with everything produced within the fog of war, there are exceptions to this, but both types were fitted with access doors at the front of the body on each side thus giving four *formal* entry and exit points.

Disembarkation in a hurry, of course, meant that over the sides and over the (still-closed) tailboard became informal exit points and Sam King, formerly a Sergeant in the AEC whilst attached to 5 Bn RASC (in 1948, before it was graced with the title *Royal* Army Education Corps), recalls how the jump could, indeed, be a 'giant leap for mankind'! The weight of an infantryman's kit, together with the impetus of the jump, was often enough to throw one off balance. This is easy enough to understand when it is realized that the deck height was around 4ft, and the closed tailboard height over 6ft high, depending on how heavily laden the vehicle was.

The overall length of the QLT was 21ft 10in compared with the QLD's 19ft 8in. This allowed an additional 3ft 5¼in – including the space vacated by the petrol tank and spare wheel – on the body length so that it could accommodate, altogether, 30 troops seated, with all their kit, plus the driver; 29 of them 'inside' and one 'up front' who had the added responsibility of taking care of any action required from the AA hatch immediately above his head.

The QLT was slightly shorter than the QLD, at 9ft 8in overall, and

A convoy of QLD troop carriers, near Portsmouth. Note the censor's change of mind, with the mark 'stet', in allowing this photo to be produced even with the wing-plate stating NOT FOR SHIPMENT. The hatching out across the building is to prevent too-easy identification of the precise location.

its shipping height was only 7ft 6in. Inside the extended body the length was 15ft 10in; the width was 7ft 1½in and the interior height was exactly 6ft. Total gross weight was 6 ton 11cwt, with the front axle carrying 2 ton 6cwt and the rear axle 4 ton 5cwt.

The Trooper could be used for carrying loads as well as personnel and, indeed, was popular in this role because of the extra body space it offered. Use in load-carrying mode entailed folding back, flat, the side seats and removing the centre seat-assembly which could then be stowed in a recess under the floor of the body. Standing instructions were that the load should be carried well forward, but it was pointless asking a part-load of troops to sit well forward as they always wanted to sit at the tail, to see what was going on! The reasons for loading well forward are simple. First, with the load placed too far aft, traction and steering effort was reduced on the front axle. Second, the extension to the chassis could not be relied upon for continued use with heavy weights – either being dropped on to the tail end whilst loading and before being moved into place within the body, or driven over rough surfaces. This fact was apparent on some vehicles which had seen very hard service where repeated boarding and disembarking of troops across the tail had caused it to sag a little – hence its affectionate name, the QL 'Drooper'.

Contracts for the QLT include V4675, placed in July 1941 for 1,050

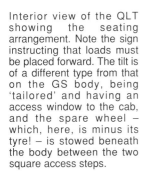

Interior view of the QLT showing the seating arrangement. Note the sign instructing that loads must be placed forward. The tilt is of a different type from that on the GS body, being 'tailored' and having an access window to the cab, and the spare wheel – which, here, is minus its tyre! – is stowed beneath the body between the two square access steps.

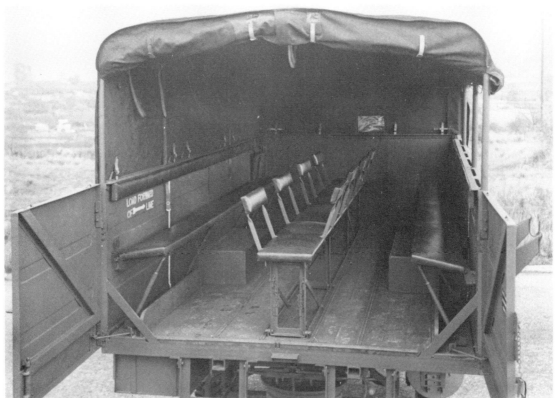

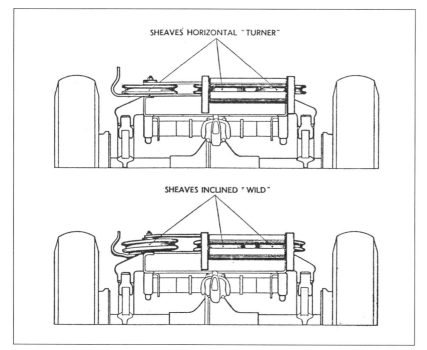

SHEAVES HORIZONTAL "TURNER"

SHEAVES INCLINED "WILD"

How to identify the two types of winch gear fitted to the QLB and, later, to the QLW. In practice, identification was easier than the diagram suggests; the problem was remembering exactly which was which, although when it came to using the winch it made little difference, there being proponents of both types.

'QLC for modification to QLT', with the chassis extension being added by the body-builder, Austin. The contract was annotated with the cryptic comment 'details from Colclough', the meaning of which has been lost in the mists of time. The vehicles were supplied at a chassis/cab price of £359.16.0d and the troop carrying body added a further £186.12.8d to make a total of £546.8.8d. Delivery was scheduled to start in August 1941 and to continue through to August the following year, with the RASC receiving 800 and the RAOC the other 250. Being an early contract, WD numbers were allocated at the time the Army received the vehicles so the RASC had numbers L557230 to L558029 except L557654 (a total of 799 vehicles), and the RAOC had numbers L4591022 to L4591271 plus L4591409, a total of 251 vehicles. One is forced to wonder just how the official mind works in allocating numbers thus! The fate of at least one of these vehicles is known: L557599, renumbered after the war to 61RE86, was posted to the RASC in BAOR in 1968 and was probably reworked to a GS Office body.

Contract V4924 called for a further 1,500 vehicles, in two stages; first, in July 1942, for 500 and then a second bite, in February 1944, for the other 1,000. Once again, the caveat about dates being unreliable must be noted, especially as the WD numbers (L560480 to L561979) are all in one batch – and an early one at that! For some reason, the vehicle which was to have been L561930 was withdrawn and the number was not issued. Postwar, the survivors were renumbered in the range 61RE78 to 63RE21 and were intended for rework to GS Offices but numbers above 62RE23, in this batch, were not taken up. Some of the survivors were:

Vehicle	survived as	and was sent to RASC
L560513	61RE87	in BAOR in 1959
L560689	61RE92	Ashchurch
L560759	61RE91	609 MCTG[a] RCT[b] BAOR
L561044	61RE85	BAOR
L561530	61RE79	BAOR; disposed of Oct 31, 1963

[a] Mobile Civilian Transport Group
[b] Royal Corps of Transport

A QLW Winch Tipper with its tilt bows in the lowered position. The spare wheel arrangement is non-standard and the fact that this is a later (1945) model is indicated by the mudguard strengtheners. L6166501 was the first in a batch of nearly 1,000 vehicles ordered on contract number S8177 and is, in fact, the prototype, originally allocated number L5877076.

QLW

QLWs did not appear until towards the end of the war when they were widely used by the Royal Engineers for renewing defences and fortifications and for clearing debris and airfields. The prototype was constructed on a stripped-down QLB chassis, because the winch was deemed to be a useful feature in this role. It seems likely that production versions were also built from diverted or incomplete QLBs.

The driver's controls on the QLW were different from other models, even the QLB. There were *four* 'gear'-levers, the two usual ones for the main and transfer gearbox controls, plus the winch control lever, as on the QLB, and a fourth lever which controlled the hydraulics for the tipping gear, having three, notched, positions: forward to raise the body, back to lower it and the central position for when the pump was out of use.

As discussed in Chapter 4, two types of winch were available on the

One of the prototype QLWs fitted with Turner winch gear which had horizontal sheaves. This vehicle, shown here as number L6166607, was originally supplied as a QLB, number L5877076. The two hooks under the chassis, just forward of the winch, were for attaching hawsers to anchor the vehicle when engaged in very heavy winching. Although this vehicle, and L6166501, were constructed to non-APT specification, over 450 on this contract had the full APT treatment, and most would have been tropicalized as well.

QLW: the Wild gear or the Turner gear. Whilst similar in most respects, there were some little differences in the mechanical specification. On the Wild gear, the reduction gear ratio was 8.25:1 whilst that on the Turner gear, which had a slightly larger gearbox, with a capacity of 8 pints of oil compared with the Wild's 5 pints, was 8.333:1. This meant that the overall reduction from the engine, using first gear, was 60.14:1 on the former and 59.5:1 on the latter.

Both winches wound-in at the same speed, 209ft per minute, but with the Turner having a slightly shorter rope (175ft against 183 feet on the Wild), this meant *in theory* that it had the edge. The rope, which had a circumference of 2⅜in, could be wound in at

45deg each side of vehicle's centre line, or 15deg upwards and 45deg downward.

Three WD contracts were placed for this model, the first being the prototype already mentioned. Next came one for a total of 946 vehicles, most of which were non-APT. Deliveries started in December 1944 and continued at the rate of 160 per month with, in common with all later contracts, all those supplied after February 23, 1945 being to tropical specification.

WD numbers were allocated: L6166501 to L6166992 to the first 492 vehicles which were non-APT; L6166993 to L6167444 to the next 452 vehicles which *were* to APT specification and, finally, L6167445 to L6167446 to the last two vehicles which were *non*-APT, making a total of 946 vehicles. The price was £550.0.10d supplied complete with Edwards Bros tipping gear. There is, in one source, a record of an amendment dated August 11, *1946*, indicating that work may have continued on QL production after hostilities had ceased, but this is unreliable and no cross-reference has been traced.

The last contract was placed very late in the war and was cancelled before any deliveries took place against it. One thousand vehicles, allocated numbers L6255136 to L6256135 were to have been delivered from November 1945 onwards.

APT instructions – QLD and QLW

These instructions, for dismantling a complete vehicle from scratch, were supplied with the APT (air-portable) versions of the QLD GS and the QLW Winch Tipper. Some additional tasks were required for the tipper but it is clear that, in either case, this was not a job to be undertaken lightly, or in any hurry. Apart from being of interest in their own right, these instructions are a useful guide to the sequence of dismantling for restorers. Assembly is, of course, the same process in reverse.

Small wooden plugs were supplied to fit the ends of fuel and hydraulic pipes and hoses to avoid ingress of dirt and all APT vehicles were supplied with a small box of assorted spare nuts and bolts which was kept clamped to the bulkhead behind the driver. Once dismantled, the components could, allegedly, be man-handled, with the aid of fitted castors, into a Douglas DC-3 (Dakota) aircraft.

* Remove body tilt cover
* Remove and dismantle tilt cover superstructure
* Remove body tailboard
* Remove body sides and front superstructure
* Remove body fittings (chain box, POW carrier etc)
* Remove rear half of body floor
* Remove front half of body floor and body front panel
* Remove spare wheel, carrier and petrol tank assembly
* Remove top half of cab
* Remove front wings
* Reverse grab rail on LHS of cab
* Remove cab panels

* Remove sump stone guard
* Remove exhaust pipe and silencer assembly
* Remove tyre pump air filter
* Remove chassis frame sidemember extension at right hand rear
   and towing attachment
* Disconnect hydraulic brake hoses
* Disconnect handbrake cable
* Remove rear axle assembly
* Fit castor wheels
* Remove front axle assembly
* Remove road springs and wheels from front axle
* Remove body mounting brackets
* Reposition rear axle lamp and bracket
* Coat with grease all unpainted parts, including bolts and nuts
   removed during dismantling

CHAPTER 7

QLR

The QLR was the house-type model, fitted with various 'extras' including special electrical suppression, which was used for all the command and communications, and most of the office applications. There were three basic versions:

(i)   'Original'
(ii) Command (HP and LP types, Wireless)
(iii) 'New' TEV type

The original, version (i), was available with any one of a total of

Right and previous page: This QLR Type J145 Mobile Operations Room, built by Dennis Bros, was originally destined for the RAF. L5825373 was the fifth in a batch of nine which went into service in April 1944. These photographs were taken before the vehicle entered service, hence it is not yet fitted with its spare wheel or marked-up with divisional or unit markings.

A QLR Line of Communication Vehicle with House Type Wireless Body No.1 as supplied by Normand or Mann Egerton body-builders. Each of these QLR House Type bodies differed subtly in outward appearance as well as being differently equipped inside, and official records are often confused about exactly which type was which.

eight different body types. There was a Cypher Office body; a Command body which fulfilled both HP and LP roles; a Mobile Terminal Carrier; two for use as TEV (Terminal Equipment Vehicles) at both Divisional and Corps level; and three wireless bodies, for Wireless (I), Wireless (R) and Wireless HP roles.

The Command and Wireless HP models were eventually

Above, right and previous page: QLR House Type Body No.3 dating from July 1943. This vehicle is one of a large batch of 1,060 QLRs, supplied with W/T Command, Signal Office and W/T (R) bodies built by Spurlings, Mann Egerton and Mulliners.

One of an order for 250 vehicles, this QLR is fitted with the Wireless Body No.1, and was delivered in 1943. Other vehicles on this contract were fitted with either Studio – W/T (Wireless Telegraphy) or Wireless LCV (Line of Communication Vehicle) bodies.

superseded by version (ii) which, in addition to all the features fitted on version (i), had an improved L-shaped tent which could be erected along the nearside and rear of the vehicle.

The TEV type was also superseded, by version (iii), the 'new' TEV Type, which could be had either as Type A, Type B or Type C. These new TEV types had a 16ft body and were mounted on a modified chassis which embodied an extension similar to that on the QLT. A later – postwar – type (TEV Div), sometimes known as 'Body 15 (unfitted)', was similar to the 'Body 2 (unfitted)' which was, basically, the version (ii) body. The C-Type was the heaviest, weighing in at 6 ton 15cwt gross. Many of these – some of which were postwar rebuilds – soldiered on, with very low mileages, into the Seventies, which is why so many office-bodied QLs have survived. Many of these rebuilds are, for convenience, known as QLRs, since they are similar in appearance to the 'real' QLRs, even to the extent of having been fitted with generators and radio suppression equipment. However, to the purist, they remain converted QLTs!

A further role, not included above, was the Mobile Operations Room which was used by the RAF. Some of these, of which 'local' interpretations of design and specification appear to exist, were not QLRs but house-bodied QLCs – just to add to the general confusion!

The eight wireless body types which were available to the Army up to 1945 were also often confused, even in official circles, because the differences between them were quite subtle. As an example of this confusion and the extent to which 'dialect' names sprang up, the bodies called for on one contract, dated June 1942, are variously referred to as 'Studio W/T' (Wireless Telegraphy), 'House Type No.1' and 'Wireless LCV' (Line of Communication Vehicle). References to this order appear in many other sources and amongst the other descriptions applied are QLR W/B 143in (variously interpreted as meaning 'Wireless Body Type 143' and as 'Wheelbase 143' – which is, of course, the QL's wheelbase dimension!) Others include 'HP Type K, c/w/wireless' and 'Cypher Office – Medium – unfitted'. Other documents refer to 'Type K', 'Type 10 Cypher Office', 'Type 8 R & I', 'Type 9 T.E.V. Div & Corps', 'Command HP' and 'W/T Body 8 U/F R & I'. No wonder there was confusion! Some of this batch, allocated numbers L4919331 to L4919580, saw service with 21 AG (21st Army Group, which became BAOR) in north-west Europe in 1945 and one of them was supplied to the RAOC, possibly for experimental purposes.

Mechanically, the QLR was much the same as other models but, in addition, had – for its time – fairly sophisticated radio suppression equipment on the ignition distributor and spark plugs so that sparks from these components would not interfere with radio reception and transmission. They were also fitted with a pto, from the rear of the transfer gearbox to the special 660 watt auxiliary dynamo, the control for which was situated in the cab, to the left of the main gear-lever. To engage the drive, the driver had to depress the clutch pedal, engage top gear in the main gearbox and pull the pto lever right back, having first ensured that all the auxiliary electrical equipment had been connected.

Equipment varied between roles but was very comprehensive. For example, in the wireless role, the internal, or Staff, section of the body was fitted with a full-width, double-sided map-board and on the offside door there was a hinged table. Also in this compartment

A QLR of the later 'new' TEV type body, fitted on to an extended chassis. This one has the HT TEV body Type B, built by Mulliners. Postwar, many surviving QLTs were converted to this role. Other vehicles on the same contract were fitted with Type 15 bodies and there were also some 13ft Shell Container lorries supplied.

was a full-width desk for three men and a sliding glass window in the partition. Seating consisted of a revolving seat with a folding stand for the commander and, for the other staff, there were two sliding seats with lockers and a further folding seat.

In the Operations section of the body there was another full-width operator's desk plus two operators' seats, each with stowage

The House Body TEV (Terminal Equipment Vehicle) No.15 for the QLR was a later version than the No.3, there having been no intermediate numbers! This one, supplied in tropicalized and APT format, dates from 1944.

Most of this batch of 26 QLRs went to the RAF with Type J145 Mobile Ops Room bodies built by Dennis Bros and were delivered urgently "at the expense of other contracts" in November 1943. This one, however, had the Type S106 body and dates from February 1944.

Interior of a QLR Command HP Body No.1 Wireless vehicle showing the cramped working conditions. With a crew of six, or more, and all the radio equipment on, temperatures must have been quite high, even with the cooling fans activated.

underneath, and a central operator's seat with a drawer underneath it. To keep things cosy, the auxiliary engine compartment and the wireless set were also in this part of the body. Externally, the fittings included a sliding glass window in the roof, a luggage grid, two folding tables, a locker housing the tent, the vehicle's exhaust cowling, an auxiliary exhaust silencer, a roof ladder, cowlings for the 12-volt extractor fans, a louvred grille for the fan in the wireless set, stowage for engine ramps and aerial masts, a full-width kit locker and further locker units to house three cable drums and eight batteries, non-skid chains, and a 20-gallon drinking-water container! There was also a rectifier box, fuel for the auxiliary engine, a jerrican, a fourth cable drum, and an oil can.

The tent, which could be erected at the rear of the vehicle, was initially supplied for Wireless (R) applications only but was later added as standard equipment on the other types.

The dimensions of the various models and types differed slightly: the 'Original' was 20ft 6in long, the 'New' type was 6in shorter, at 20ft exactly, whilst the 'New TEV' was 22ft 3in in length. They were all about the same width, at 7ft 6in, although some of the earlier 'Originals' were 7ft 7in in width. In height they varied from 9ft 4in to 10ft exactly. Inside the body, taking version (ii) as an example, the front compartment was 6ft 3in long; the rear one 6ft 3½in long. It was 6ft 8in in width and had headroom of 5ft 3in.

As for weights, taking version (i) as an example, this weighed, unladen, without its signals or any vehicle equipment, 3 ton 19cwt 1qtr all up, with 1 ton 19cwt 3qtr on the front axle and 1 ton 19cwt 2qtr on the back. In its heaviest role, Wireless HP, this increased, laden, to 6 ton 16cwt 1qtr, gross.

By comparison, the Command HP E 53 version, the heaviest role

A QLR Line of Communication Vehicle shown with its crew busy erecting the aerials. This model has the House Type Wireless Body No.1 and is of the type supplied by Mann Egerton and Normand. It seems likely that this one is on trials since it is not carrying a census number.

carried out by the QLR, unladen weight was increased to 4 ton 19cwt 3qtr and all-up gross weight was 7 ton 10cwt, the theoretical design maximum for the vehicle. This was distributed with, on the front axle 2 ton 18cwt 1qtr and, on the rear axle 4 ton 11cwt 3qtr.

Many firms were engaged in the production of bodies for the QLR, amongst which were companies such as Brush Coachworks, Carbodies, Car Cruiser Caravans, Dennis, Elliott, Mann Egerton, Mulliners, Normand, Park Royal, Spurlings and Strachans. Dennis Brothers manufactured horseboxes and similar equipment in peacetime, and should not be confused with the Guildford-based company, famous for fire engines and, later, municipal vehicles, who were engaged on other war work. Mulliners built large numbers of office and house-type box bodies for QLs and, in some cases the WD contract was placed direct with them, often simply for 'QLR bodies' – type unspecified.

Spurling Motor Bodies had, during and shortly after the war, seven branches, with headquarters at Hendon. The company was set up in 1928 and specialized in building bodies for commercial vehicles, soon becoming the biggest General Motors dealer in the country. The company has now changed hands but the successor to the old firm, which is still known as Spurlings, continues to receive requests for spares for vehicles which were originally supplied 50 years ago. An odd example amongst these was a request for spares for a set of motorized aircraft steps which, when supplied, were known as the Spurmobile!

The QLR body was prototyped by Car Cruiser Caravans. Allocated WD number L5509984, this was the most expensive QLR ever built, with the chassis/cab costing a fairly standard £429.9.7d but the prototype body costing £765.10.11d, making a total vehicle price of £1,195.0.6d! Following successful prototyping, a whole batch of production contracts was placed with Bedford on October 17, 1942.

Two of these called for a total of 900 vehicles, at a chassis/cab price of £401.4.11d. Deliveries against this contract, some of which had

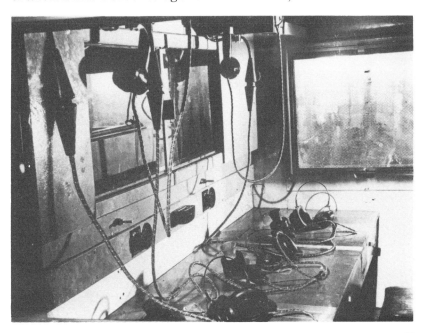

Interior view of a QLR built to LWR Wireless specification showing the radio operators' headsets on the bench behind the front bulkhead.

One of a batch of 180 QL Offices built by Elliotts on QLC chassis showing how the tent was erected to extend the working area. Later deliveries in this batch — those after chassis number 47038 — were built to the full APT specification; earlier ones were APT except for the towing bar, which was fabricated in one piece instead of two.

More difficult to identify than some (!) this QLR House Type, completely enshrouded in its extension tent, has a No.3 Body and shows an alternative tent configuration to that shown with L5877091. Many different tent versions were available and it is not unlikely that there was quite a degree of local 'custom building' and other adaptation as well.

'W/T Cmnd Type 143' bodies built by Mann Egerton, were required at the rate of 60 to 70 per month, starting in February 1943. Orders for the remainder were placed with two different body-builders: Spurlings built 200 'Cmnd Wireless' bodies and Mulliners supplied the remainder as 'House Type A GS Wireless HP53 unfitted'.

In addition to the Army types available, the RAF had several designs of their own. The J Type, of which three versions could be had – Types 102, 103 and 106 – was the basic RAF 'Signals' body. The other main RAF type was the 'Type 145, Mobile Ops Room', which incorporated double walls with insulating panels on a wooden frame. On this version, the gap between the cab and the body was often filled by a compartment erected above the spare wheel and some versions even had a 'Luton' extension above the cab.

A postwar photograph of a QLR Terminal Equipment Vehicle crew setting up their equipment. Of interest, particularly on a vehicle having survived the war, is the absence of wheel-hub flanges – usually a sign of early production. Note, also, that the 'Mickey Mouse' camouflage has been retained.

The official drawing of the QL LCV in its High-Power Wireless Station role seems an unnecessarily elaborate way of instructing which aerial is of which type. However, it is typical of contemporary drawings and is of interest in its own right.

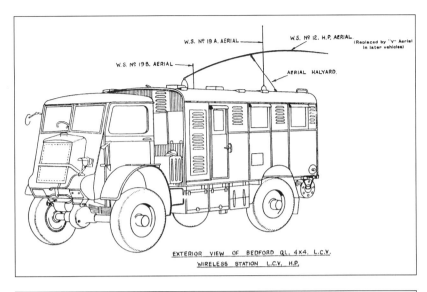

EXTERIOR VIEW OF BEDFORD QL, 4x4, L.C.V.
WIRELESS STATION L.C.V, H.P.

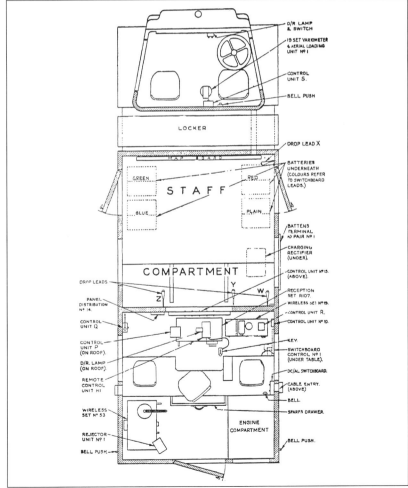

By contrast, the plan diagram is very informative and shows just how cramped working conditions must have been in the Command – Wireless HP – Ground Station, referenced as Cmnd – HP/12 HP/19.

95

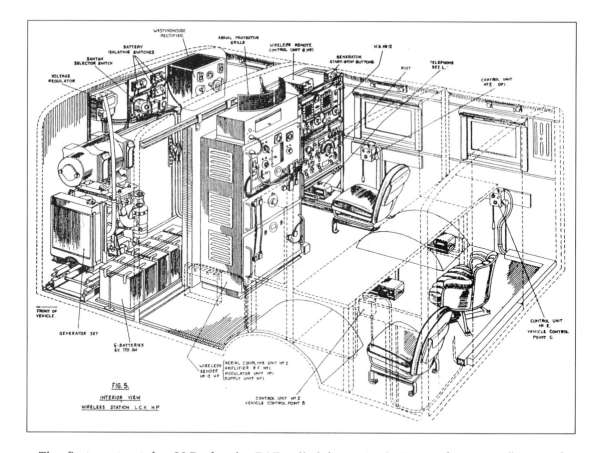

Within the figure:
WESTINGHOUSE RECTIFIER.
AERIAL PROTECTIVE GRILLE
BATTERY ISOLATING SWITCHES
WIRELESS REMOTE CONTROL UNIT @ N°1.
W.S. N° 12
SANTON SELECTOR SWITCH
GENERATOR START-STOP BUTTONS
TELEPHONE SET L.
VOLTAGE REGULATOR
R107
CONTROL UNIT N° 2. OP 1
FRONT OF VEHICLE.
GENERATOR SET
G-BATTERIES 6V. 170 AH
WIRELESS SENDER N° 12 H.P
AERIAL COUPLING UNIT N° 2
AMPLIFIER R.F N°1
MODULATOR UNIT N°1
SUPPLY UNIT N°1
CONTROL UNIT N° 2 VEHICLE CONTROL POINT B
CONTROL UNIT N° E VEHICLE CONTROL POINT C.

FIG. 5.
INTERIOR VIEW
WIRELESS STATION L.C.V. H.P

The first contract for QLRs for the RAF called for a single QLC chassis/cab 'for mounting of prototype Signals body (QLR)'. The body for this particular vehicle was built by Mulliners, as a 'Signals Type 145', although various sources also refer to it as being a Type 102 and as a Type 103, 'similar to RAF Signals Types supplied by Dennis Bros', presumably, as this was a prototype, on other chassis including possibly Crossley or Thornycroft. The contract was placed on July 9, 1943, calling for delivery in August and that neither Bedford nor Mulliners wasted any time is indicated by its being into the paint shops on August 4! The chassis/cab cost £352.10.6d and the body (listed as a *Dennis* signals body) cost £357.1.1.d giving a total cost for this prototype of £709.11.7d. This was followed by production orders on a number of contracts. S4658, of October 7, 1943, called for 23 vehicles to be supplied to the RAF with J Type 145 Mobile Ops Room bodies built by Dennis Bros and numbers L5455220 to L54555242. These, too, were needed in a hurry and, to achieve the required date, Bedford were instructed to deliver 'at the expense of other contracts'. This batch cost £414.18.5d for the chassis/cab and £355.7.4d for the body, a total of £770.5.9d.

Next, on December 4, 1943, came 29 vehicles again with J-Type 145 Mobile Ops Room bodies built by Dennis Bros. These were required by February 1943, at the expense of other contracts which

A cutaway diagram of a Line of Communication Vehicle fitted with what is believed to be a Wireless set No.53.

96

Lt Gen Sir M C Dempsey KCB DSO MC, Commander, 2nd Army, about to enter his caravan HQ – and at his desk in the caravan office in January 1945.

A group of Line of Communications Vehicles tucked away so as to be as much out of harm's way as was possible, in February 1945. Each vehicle was in communication with one of the major cities in the UK, providing a constant channel of two-way communication.

called for a mixture of QLCs, QLTs and QL Signals Control Cabins, totalling 2,000 vehicles. This priority order ultimately resulted in 650 other vehicles simply being cancelled. The 29, which cost £422.19.0d for the chassis/cab and £354.19.0d for the body (total £777.18.0d) were allocated numbers L5518353 to L5518381. Another contract called for a further nine vehicles, numbers L5825368 to L5825376 with similar details, having Type J145 Dennis Bros bodies, plus a hitherto unknown type, the J140.

An order for 26 QLRs for delivery in January and February 1945 was, for some unknown reason, cancelled. Their WD numbers had been allocated (L5869841 to L5869866) and the price was known – £370.9.5d for the chassis/cab and £480 for the Mulliners body. At £850.9.5d these would have been the most expensive production QLR to date and perhaps gives the clue to their cancellation.

Other QLR contracts include a considerable miscellany of partially complete, contradictory and apparently inaccurate records. There are, however, some interesting titbits to emerge.

Contract S5907, placed in February 1944, calls for a total of 651 QLRs, of which 12 are decidedly special. These dozen vehicles were fitted with special armoured bodies for RA staff vehicles under a separate contract of which the only details which can be traced are that numbers L6171625 to L6171636 were allocated. For the remaining standard versions, two body-builders were used: Spurling, who fitted LP Type A Wireless 3 Unfitted bodies; and Mulliner, who supplied unfitted bodies types 6 and 8.

Finally, a contract of particular interest is one for a fairly late modification built on the QLT chassis – so, as already discussed, these were not strictly QLRs at all even though their appearance was broadly similar to the 'new' TEV type. They were, in fact, designated 'WD Caravan for Senior Officers' and provided, for wartime conditions, extraordinarily good accommodation. To the QLT chassis were added a fixed roof and sides and the interior was divided into two sections – one for sleeping and living, the other for working, facilities also being provided for the officer to work in the open air if he preferred, for which a side and rear tent were provided; the tailboard folded down to make a working platform in this mode. Within the living quarters were a bed measuring 2ft 10in by 6ft 10in together with a wash-basin and a dressing table, an assortment of cupboards and a mirror. The living area was curtained-off from the working area which contained a desk on the left-hand side, facing which, on the opposite wall, was a softwood map-board panel. The caravan was well stocked with equipment, too, having a 30-gallon drinking-water tank, with a hand-operated pump and 110-volt lighting backed up by emergency lighting by batteries. The whole vehicle measured 21ft long, 7ft 2in wide and 10ft high in its 'transport mode'. The Bedford production for this model was priced at £386.13.8d and bodies were supplied by Eccles. Numbers allocated were L5585864 to L5585903.

The last QLR contract of all, for 240 vehicles (L6238913 to L6239152) to be delivered from August 1945 onwards, whilst cancelled, had a note pinned to it: "One on charge awaiting confirmation." This note is dated January 4, 1946 – another indication that work may have been done on QLs after the end of the war.

CHAPTER 8

Postwar

In contrast with the war years when few, if any, details were released about the QL – or about any other military equipment, for that matter – the postwar period saw a flood of information becoming available. Many newspapers published war histories, old soldiers, sailors and airmen published their memoirs and, as has already been seen in Chapter 2, even the professional institutes discussed publicly the specifications for wartime equipment. Joining in this feast of information dissemination was Vauxhall's distributor network newspaper, *The Vauxhall and Bedford News* which, by the time of the November/December 1945 issue, considered it quite safe to make public at least some details.

The first article to discuss the topic of QLs concerned how the APT versions of the QLW and the QLD GS came about. It revealed how the initial inquiry from the War Department came as late as 1944 and how Bedford immediately started discussions with the Army Airborne Transport Development Centre, at Amesbury. It went on to describe how the specification was worked up so that a Douglas DC–3, the famous Dakota, would be able to carry two APT-dismantled QLs. Having owned an APT QLD, and having flown in a Dakota, the author is inclined to believe that this must have been an extremely tight fit! Photographs were also included with the article, portraying the fully dismantled vehicle, but not showing how it fitted into the aircraft.

Throughout the war years, Vauxhall had kept in touch with their distributors with a wartime economy version of the newspaper for their distributors as well as one for their workforce – *The Vauxhall Mirror*. They had also been very active in printing other material. Each vehicle had been supplied with a driver's handbook and a service manual. Foreign language versions were also made available as QLs were deployed with non English-speaking allies. In June 1941, Vauxhall produced a booklet for Bedford mechanics which the authorities thought to be so good that it was used as a training guide on *all* vehicle types.

In February 1941, they produced an initial run of 10,000 copies of a little booklet called *For B.F.s*. This was specifically written for 'the other fellow', as it contained advice on driving and maintenance which was of the very simplest nature, but which covered the sort of topics generally forgotten, such as daily checks, lubrication and a host of other gentle reminders – including remembering to push in the choke control! – all written in a friendly and humorous way. By October 1944, 200,000 copies of the booklet had been distributed and it is now a collector's item.

At one time during the war, in an endeavour to keep the Bedford family in touch, *The Vauxhall and Bedford News* published a regular listing of where their training instructors were deployed. This rapidly became quite a serious security risk as Bedford instructors were to be seen in almost every theatre of the war and publication gave away far too much about troop positions.

Of the greatest interest in these newspapers, at least to the enthusiast, were the references to QLs. Bedford seemed to be very proud of their product, but were unable to say too much about it during the war years, for security reasons. In the April 1942 edition of the *News* the first photograph of a QL appeared, but it was very carefully obscured for the casual reader by the title! It appeared again, in that year's August edition, but it was still obscured by text. By October, the first unobscured photograph appeared, but it was of a QL a long way back in a general convoy – so it was still virtually impossible to find any detail about them. However, in February 1943, official clearance must have been given, for not only did a proper photograph appear on the front cover, but the vehicle was the subject of the main article in the paper. It was also the major topic in a further article in the June 1944 edition which showed L4483166 – a QLB from the very first contract ever issued for QLs – as well as another QL filling-in on civilian service on bus route 73 in London! Battlefield scenes showing QLs appeared in the October and December 1944 editions. In the February 1945 edition a *Radio Times* article was reprinted about MCO broadcasting from a QL in Normandy, and the June/July edition had coverage of the beach landings in which QLs, as has been seen, figured largely. The August 1945 edition shows the *Luftwaffe*'s map of the Luton works where QLs were produced, as well as photos of the Luton factory's bomb damage.

By the end of the war, QLs had seen active service in virtually every land campaign since the time of its becoming available to the armed forces. This included action – in alphabetical order, to avoid any suggestion of an order of importance – in Antwerp, Bremen, Brussels, Burma, El Alamein, Hamburg, Monte Cassino, Normandy, the crossings of the Po, Rhine and Seine rivers, Salerno, Sicily, Tripoli and Tunisia and, more than likely, many other, possibly less well-known actions as well. The vehicle's remarkable qualities, and the sheer numbers in which they were produced, meant that they

Axles from scrapped QLs finding a second career as lifting jacks with Frank Annis & Co in the heavy haulage industry. The jacks illustrated were capable of lifting 60 tons: other versions could lift 100 tons – very slowly! Here they are shown lifting the barge *Cleopatra* before it was transported by road, to the studios where it featured in a film.

continued in military service for many years after World War Two, and not only in the British armed forces, where they saw further service in Trieste (1945-54), Java/Sumatra (1945), Greece (1945-47), the Canal Zone and Egypt (1946-54), India (1945-48), Palestine (1945-48), Aden (1947), Korea (1950-53), Cyprus (1954-59), Hong Kong (1956), Suez (1956) and many other postings, remaining in service long after its successor, the Bedford RL 3/4-tonner, was introduced in 1952.

Many QLs had also been supplied to the Allies and continued in their operational fleets for years to come. Those which stayed with the British forces were renumbered with the now familiar 99AA99 style of numbering (Appendix 2) and were either refurbished by a complete overhaul, converted to some other use or disposed of into the civilian sector which was, of course, hungry for general transport vehicles of any description.

Large quantities of spares also survived the conflict and Bedford continued to support the model range for many years – it is possible to obtain most engine spares, even today – particularly as the engine was, essentially, common to the MW, OX and OY model ranges as well as to all the various civilian models which survived the war and the new ones slowly becoming available, though mostly for export, it has to be said!

The Base Workshop overhauls, which were carried out by REME, were completed to a very high standard, which probably accounts for why so many have survived into the Nineties in preservation. The conversions were of several types: many surplus Troopers were converted to Office types, designated 'New TEV Type' as seen in Chapter 7.

All, or most, of the surviving 6-pounder Anti-Tank Portees were converted to General Service use, but retained the canvas cab-top, and surpluses of other types were either stripped of their original bodies and refitted with General Service bodies or were converted to something akin to a GS role. Just after the war, D Claridge, who started the war *building* QLs and ended up driving them with 75 Anti-Tank Regiment, recalls being sent to large vehicle dump at Venlo, in Holland, to recover and make good two QLs for conversion into buses (TCVs). Once made serviceable, he says, they were as reliable as when they were first built.

In many cases, though, the cost of bringing back vehicles, some of them very much the worse for wear, from far-flung postings was such that it was, on occasion, seen to be more economic to load them into landing craft, take them out to sea and simply push them overboard. This seems, to the enthusiastic admirer of QLs, to be a heart-breaking reward for loyal service from a vehicle, but inevitably, economics come before sentiment.

For the men and women who served in the forces during the war, loyal service was rewarded by the presentation of a variety of campaign and commemorative medals and decorations. If medals had been awarded to the equipment which served these men and women, it is salutary to think that the QL would have qualified for almost a complete set, plus those from the many postwar overseas postings, quite apart from those awarded by other, allied forces. All campaign and commemorative medals for World War Two are listed in Appendix 3.

Once peace had been restored, the QL found a warm welcome when it became available to the civilian market as War Surplus. Bert Coleman, who drove Bren Carriers during the war had, as his first peacetime job, the task of transporting loads of hay from the verdant pastures of south-east Surrey to the Horlicks farm in Wiltshire. His recollection is of the degree to which overloading was prevalent – Vauxhall used to advertise that Bedfords were built for a 50 per cent overload. He also remembers, particularly, the lack of pace they could demonstrate climbing the long drag on what is now the A303 – hardly surprising with a 50 per cent overload! Contemporary advertisements show QLs being offered as 5-tonners for load carrying and, indeed, they were a popular buy at £95 each with "...cheap spares, engines, gearboxes, axles etc. Enquiries invited!"

QLs were, though, used in many guises apart from straightforward load carrying. They can be seen in old photographs as 'wreckers', or breakdown and recovery vehicles – one was used as the recovery vehicle at the 1948 Silverstone Grand Prix – as mobile show caravans, and by the electricity and telephone authorities as pole carriers, converted to dropsiders.

Retired tankers and bowsers were widely used, especially in quarrying work where their off-road ability was invaluable. QLs also worked in quarries in their own right as load carriers, and as timber 'nibs' and forestry extraction vehicles. Bodies were converted to flat platforms, to stakesided waggons and dropsides and even to buses, where one example was operated by the local municipal authority, Southport Corporation, taking sightseers over the sands at Morecambe Bay. QLs were also used in gathering sea-coal, the coal which is washed ashore from seams lying out to sea, from the beaches in the Hartlepool area. In spite of this very hostile environment in which the vehicles were frequently driven into the sea, some of them lasted well into the Eighties.

Even the bits and pieces from scrapped QLs had second careers. Roger Annis, of the heavy haulage firm, Frank Annis & Co, tells of the use of old QL axles converted to tower jacks. The first such set was used for moving the barge *Cleopatra* to Elstree film studios and was reported in *Commercial Motor*. The jacks, capable of lifting some 60 tons, consisted of a winding handle fixed to the input shaft of the differential, with a sprocket on the halfshaft driving a pinion on a parallel shaft with a saddle atop the whole device. Gearing could be altered by changing the differential ratios and one set was made up to be capable of lifting 100 tons. The gearing on this set needed 100 turns of the handle to raise the load one inch; two men would each wind their 100 turns and then change shifts!

Sadly, of course, many QLs were scrapped but quite a few survived into preservation. Keith Jenkinson's book, *Preserved Military Vehicles*, published in 1983, lists 47 in conservation including QLBs,

Some of the derelicts which can still be found around the country, just waiting for a sympathetic restorer. This photo shows a QLD with a House Body and added water tanks – possibly for use as a mobile clinic, and a QLR with a No.3 Body. Examples like these can still be found and, if not rescued soon, will deteriorate to the extent that they cannot be economically saved.

QLC Tankers and AT Portees, lots of QLD GS, QLR Wireless, Office, Command Post, Signals and even a Machine Shop, QLT Troopers and a number of unspecified models, and this list is certainly very far from complete. There appear to be no records of QLC Artics surviving into preservation, which is a pity since they were of considerable interest. Similarly, there are no records of some of the less common bodies like field kitchens surviving although there is a 'prophylactic' in the Museum of Army Transport, at Beverley, Humberside. Constant searching has unearthed a number of derelicts awaiting attention including QLRs, QLCs with house-type bodies and at least one fire tender, sadly neglected and with 'alien' tyres.

Only a few years ago the author was involved with the rescue of an airfield refueller, which had lain untouched for many years at the back of a barn near the airfield it had once served. A check on the oil level in the sump and a gallon or so of water to top-up the level in the radiator, a couple of gallons of petrol in the tank and a set of jump-leads had it started in no time – yet another tribute to Bedford's engineering and to the RAF who must have looked after it so well.

With such a large initial availability of good quality vehicles and with 'wrecks' still being found around the country, together with fairly readily available spares, QLs are not too difficult a restoration task. Cannibalization is already fairly commonplace as the best parts were saved from damaged vehicles and re-used. If in doubt about whether to have a go at restoring, or even just simply keeping and caring for, an old QL – or any other antique vehicle for that matter – just do it. The rewards, in terms of enjoyment and satisfaction, are tremendous.

Take care not to pay over the odds as there are those who are only involved in preservation for what they see as investment reasons. This is a great pity as their greed tends to spoil it for those who really love and care for old vehicles and simply wish to see them preserved as reminders of a past era in road transport. Joining a preservation club is a good idea, even before you purchase a vehicle of your own – it puts you in touch with like-minded people as well as with vast stores of knowledge and experience. In the author's view, public auctions of historic vehicles should be avoided at all costs as they attract the investors and drive up prices to almost ludicrous levels.

If at all possible, keep your vehicle under cover. Not only will it deteriorate less quickly when covered up, but it is also out of sight from prying – and thieving – eyes. Annual Road Tax (for QLs being constructed before January 1, 1947) is only £60 per year at the time of writing, and fully comprehensive insurance, for the limited mileage which is likely to be covered, is about the same amount. Fuel must be standard 4-star (leaded) petrol 'diluted' at a ratio of 20:1 petrol to diesel, to lower the octane rating. If you have never driven a large vehicle before, do take the trouble to have someone train you in its handling. It is senseless to venture forth on today's roads in an elderly and, by modern standards, slightly unpredictable, vehicle with no power steering and a crash gearbox to think about, if you have not handled anything larger than a Transit. You do not actually need an LGV licence, but a spot of LGV training would certainly repay itself.

One last word which relates to QLs and vehicles of similar age.

These vehicles are, by a special concession, exempt from MOT tests and from plating and testing. This does not mean that they are exempt from on-the-spot inspections and, if your vehicle is found to be unroadworthy, there is hell to pay – and quite rightly so. It is your responsibility, and should be your pleasure, to ensure that your beautifully restored vehicle not only looks absolutely right, but that it *is* absolutely right in the eyes of the law and other road users.

Two more views of the author's much-loved QLD GS APT. The '49' marking denotes 49 Field Park Unit, which worked in support of 48, 50 and 51 Field Units. These units were engaged, immediately after D-Day, at the eastern extremity of Sword Beach, working in the Ouistreham area. After the war this vehicle saw service in Cyprus, registered 43 YW 60.

APPENDIX 1

Technical specification - QL

QLs were fitted with the 'improved', Bedford '28hp' six-cylinder petrol engine which had a 85.73mm bore and 101.6mm stroke, giving a capacity of 3,518cc (214.7cu in). Known as the '28hp' engine, its RAC rating was, in fact, 27.34hp. This unit gave a maximum output of 72bhp at 3,000rpm, but the engine was usually governed to 2,500rpm at which the output was 68bhp. The maximum torque of 1,944lb.in (162lb.ft) was developed at 1,200rpm. The cooling system was of 29 pints capacity.

Suspension was by semi-elliptic springs with hydraulic double-acting shock absorbers at both the front and the rear. The foot-brake was vacuum servo-assisted on all wheels and the handbrake was mechanical, acting on the rear wheels only. Steering gear was of the worm-and-sector type and tyres were 10.5 x 20in Dunlop Trak-Grip Cross Country. It is interesting to note that many restored QLs are fitted with 11.5 x 20in or other 'adapted' tyres, owing to the difficulty of obtaining the genuine article so, for purists, this is a good point to watch for!

The QL's transmission consisted of a 10in diameter single-dry-plate clutch and the main gearbox, which was of the 'crash' type, had four forward gears and one reverse. An auxiliary, or 'transfer' gearbox, with two speeds, effectively doubled this up. The transfer box ratios were: high-ratio drive: 1.185:1 and low-ratio drive: 2.292:1. Axles, both at the front and at the rear were of the fully floating type; the final drive was via Bendix Tracta universal joints to the spiral-bevel differential whose ratio was 37:6 (6.167:1).

The ratios and speeds for each of the gears were as follows:

	Main gearbox	Overall – high ratio	mph	Overall – low ratio	mph
First	7.22	52.76	5	102.05	3
Second	3.47	25.36	11	49.03	6
Third	1.71	12.50	22	24.17	11
Top	Direct	7.31	38	14.13	20
Reverse	7.15	52.25	5	101.06	3

The general dimensions of the QL were, for the most part, the same as for the standard General Service model. These varied little across the various types and, where differences *did* occur, they are mentioned in the appropriate chapter. The general dimensions were:

Turning circle:	55ft	0in
Length:	19ft	8½in
Track – front:	5ft	8in
– rear:	5ft	6½in
Width:	7ft	5in
Wheelbase:	11ft	11in
Ground clearance:	1ft	0in

The unladen weight of the QLD was 3 ton 4cwt 2qtr and, laden, this increased to 6 ton 17cwt 2qtr.

Other details of the QL specification which are of interest concern the fuel tanks. This was a single 28-gallon tank behind the cab on the nearside on models QLB, QLD, QLR and QLW. On models QLC and QLT there were twin 16-gallon tanks which were slung under the body on either side. On the single tank versions, a fuel cut-off tap was fitted on top of the tank which had a reserve tank feature. The tap was pulled out to draw on the main tank and then pulled out again as far as it would go, and twisted, to draw on the reserve supply of about 4 gallons. On the twin-tank versions, the main tap was on the right hand (offside) of the vehicle, just in front of the tank; the fuel tap here was pulled out to draw on the right-hand tank and pushed in to draw on the left-hand one which was fitted with a similar tap to the single tank versions.

It has already been seen that the QL was no 'racer'. Its performance gave a maximum speed, with the engine ungoverned, of 48mph. However, the engine was invariably governed, thus restricting speed to 38mph. Recommended convoy speed was 25mph, at which the QL behaves very sedately and is a total joy to drive. With 50-year-old restorations, the achievement of 38mph is quite exciting enough! Overall, the power available was 10.6bhp per ton and tractive effort per ton, at 100 per cent, was 1,490lb.

APPENDIX 2

Numbering and prefixing

Until the outbreak of war, and for a short while afterwards, the first two digits of the Census Number indicated the year in which the vehicle entered service, but with the vast number of vehicles needed once war had begun, this system had to be abandoned.

After the war, the old WD or Census Numbering system was discontinued and replaced with the two numbers, two letters, two numbers (99AA99) system. These allocations give a good guide to how many, and which types, of vehicles both survived the war and were retained for British forces' use.

Vehicles which were not subjected to reworking, but which were simply serviced, repaired and renumbered, were allocated numbers in the ranges 00YA01 to 99YZ99 and 00ZA01 to 99ZX99. From 00ZY01 onwards were retained for special purposes; 00RN01 to 99RN99 were allocated to the Royal Navy and most of the AA and onwards through the 'A' series were allocated to the RAF.

Amongst the non-reworked QLs was a batch in the range 00YW01 to 85YW69 which was allocated to GS Cargo vehicles, including some Fords. In this batch, the numbers from 00YW01 up to 28YW80 were never taken up so, of the 8,569 numbers allocated, only those from 28YW81 (which had been 'old' Census Number L5455740) up to 50YW60 were taken up. These were all QLD GS, amounting to a total of 2,180 vehicles (including the author's L6125561, 43YW60).

Another batch, 00YY01 to 40YY95, included GS Troop Carrying Vehicles, GS Cargo, Offices and Wireless Vehicles as well as an unspecified quantity of 4x2 Water Carriers, a Thornycroft Mobile Workshop and at least one 3-ton X-Ray vehicle, making a total of 4,095 vehicles in all. A batch of 760 LAA GS vehicles was numbered from 10YZ80 to 18YZ39 and a mixed batch of 576 vehicles, including '4x4 Bedfords', received numbers from 65ZB91 to 71ZB66. Numbers 00ZC01 to 00ZC80 was a batch of 80 GS 4x4 'Binned' vehicles and 04ZC81 to 40ZC96 was another mixed batch of 3,616 vehicles, including GS lorries 4x4 3-ton (not necessarily all Bedfords) and, finally, 67ZC53 to 75ZC04 was yet another mixed batch of 750 vehicles which included 3-ton GS – not necessarily Bedford or even 4x4.

For reworked vehicles, the series 00RB01 to 99RH99 was allocated and QLs received a long series of RE numbers as well as some in the RC series. As far as can be ascertained from surviving records, reworked QLs bore the following numbers.

From	To	Type	Quantity
78RC17	87RC16	3-ton GS Cargo	900
91RC01	91RC26	3-ton CL Battery Slave	6*
93RC60	93RC66	Fire tender	7
93RC67	93RC72	GS Kitchen	6
97RC69	97RC98	GS Tipping	30
97RC99	99RC99	GS TCV	201
59RE76	60RE47	Fuel Tanker	72
60RE48	60RE70	GS Caravan	23
61RE27	61RE60	Fire Tender	34
61RE61	61RE77	Kitchen	17
61RE78	63RE21	Office 143 numbers allocated, only 46 used	
62RE23	65RE31	numbers not taken up	309
65RE32	67RE63	Binned	232
65RE64	69RE01	TCV	338
69RE02	69RE57	Winch	56
76RE33	76RE36	LAA plus various	4

* These may have been Bedford OYs.

APPENDIX 3

Campaign and commemorative medals

The complete set of campaign and commemorative medals from World War Two is as follows:

Campaign medals
1939-45 Star
Africa Star
Aircrew Europe Star
Atlantic Star
Burma Star
France and Germany Star
Italy Star
Pacific Star

Individuals could not be awarded more than five of these medals, even if they had spent the requisite time in the region. However, there were complicated rules which permitted clasps to be worn to indicate their service.

A Burma clasp could be worn on a Pacific ribbon, and vice versa; the Atlantic Star and Aircrew Europe could be similarly 'mixed' as could the France and Germany Star and the Atlantic Star clasps. Other clasps were also issued for wearing on campaign medals, including Battle of Britain, 8th Army, North Africa 1942-43; 1st Army.

Commemorative medals
1939-45 Defence Medal; War Medal

There were also several other commemorative medals including:

Africa Service Medal
Australian Service Medal
Canadian Volunteer Service Medal
Newfoundland Volunteer War Services Medal
New Zealand War Service Medal
South African Medal for War Services
Southern Rhodesia War Service Medal

APPENDIX 4

Sources and bibliography

The following list includes many of the sources consulted whilst researching this book and is recommended for further reading. More detail is available from museums and some of the other sources listed.

Bedford, GM's British Commercial M Sedgwick – Beaulieu Books
Bedford QL Pamphlet, Conniford – Inkpen Art Productions
Bedford Vehicles & Vauxhall Cars Jan 44 – Vauxhall Motors
Bedford, You See Them Everywhere – Vauxhall Motors
Bellona Data Magazine – Bellona
Commercial Motor Road Transport L M Meyrick-Jones – Pitman
Data Book of Wheeled Vehicles Army Transport 1939-45 – HMSO
Driver's Handbook, Bedford QL – Vauxhall Motors
Driver Training, All Arms Vol II – MOD
'For B.F.s' – a handbook – Vauxhall Motors
Historic Military Vehicles Directory B H Vanderveen – ATB
History of the Royal Engineers 1939-48
Kaleidoscope of Bedford & Vauxhall Military Vehicles – Warne
Preserved Military Vehicles K Jenkinson – Rochester Press
Proceedings of the Institute of Automobile Engineers;
    1925/27/45
The Griffin Story – Vauxhall Motors

Many organizations and companies have provided information, access or help whilst compiling this record of the Bedford QL, some of which are listed below, with apologies to any who have been inadvertently omitted. Thanks are also due to those whose names appear in the text, for anecdotes and photographs.

AWD Vehicles; Public Records Office; SEME; Spurlings Ltd; Vauxhall Motors Ltd and the Imperial War Museum, the Museum of Army Transport, the REME Museum, the National Motor Museum, the RAF Museum and The Tank Museum.

APPENDIX 5

MODELLERS' PORTFOLIO

Conscious of the depth of interest in military wheeled vehicles amongst the modelling fraternity, the author and publisher are pleased to be able to reproduce on the following pages, with the kind permission of David Jane, three sets of drawings originally produced by him in 1978 for his Truck Plan series of 1:35 scale plans. They feature the Bedford QLT Troop Carrier, the QLD General Service and the QLR Wireless trucks.

All three drawings have been reproduced here at 70 per cent of their original size, which means that as printed they represent a scale of 1:50 rather than the 1:35 indicated on the drawings. Modellers wishing to obtain full-size 1:35 scale copies of these or any other drawings in David Jane's Truck Plan series can do so by writing to Lead Sled, 1f Nutts Lane, Hinckley, Leicestershire LE10 0NT.

In the hope that they will also be of interest and value to modellers, several sketches have been reproduced, with the permission of Vauxhall Motors Ltd, from the company's *Driver's Handbook for Bedford Lorry, 3-Ton, 4x4 QL models QLC-QLD-QLR-QLT*, which was issued in 1943.

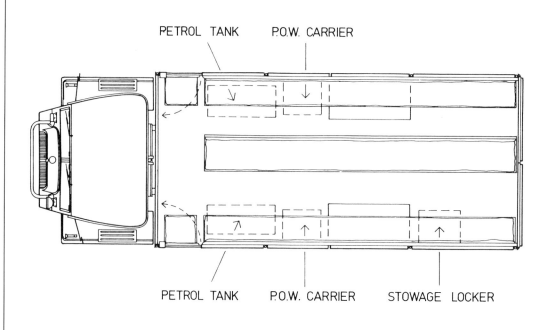

PETROL TANK　　P.O.W. CARRIER

PETROL TANK　　P.O.W. CARRIER　　STOWAGE LOCKER

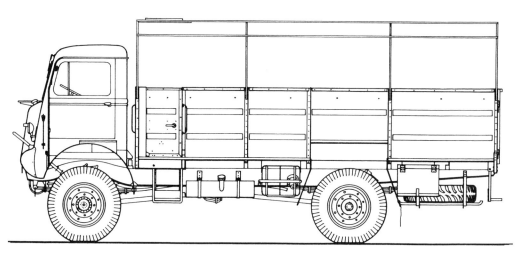

TRUCK PLAN NO. B4

BEDFORD QLT 3-ton

NOTE: Offside view shows alternative body pattern – minor differences only, within same overall dimensions.

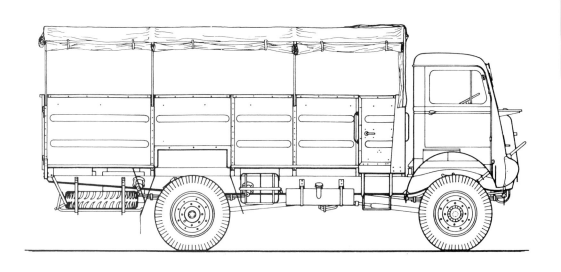

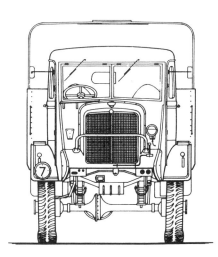

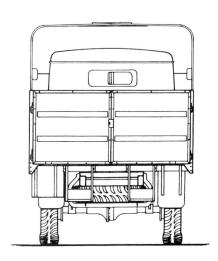

4x4 TROOP-CARRIER

SCALE 1:35

feet
metres

© DAVID E. JANE 1978

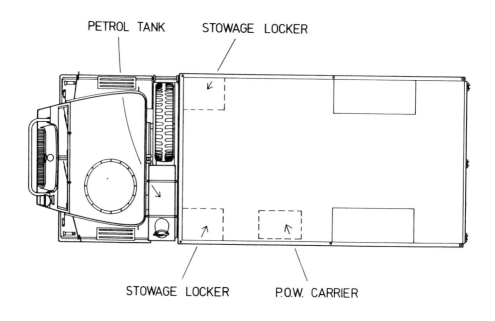

PETROL TANK   STOWAGE LOCKER

STOWAGE LOCKER   P.O.W. CARRIER

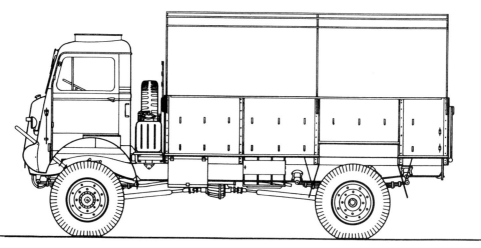

TRUCK PLAN NO. B5

BEDFORD QLD 3-ton

NOTE: Offside view shows tilt frame in the low position. Late-type split-top cab shown, with hip-ring, simpler grille layout, and mudguard strengthening brackets.

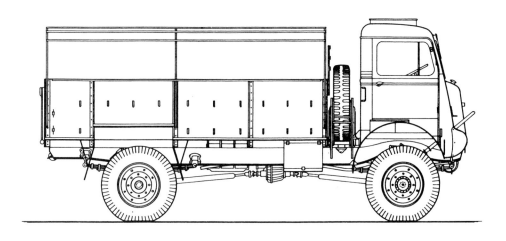

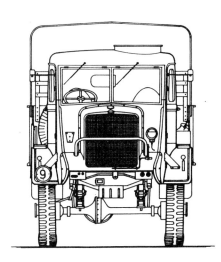

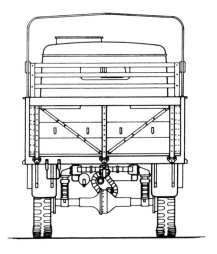

4x4 GENERAL SERVICE

SCALE 1 35

feet
metres

© DAVID E. JANE 1978

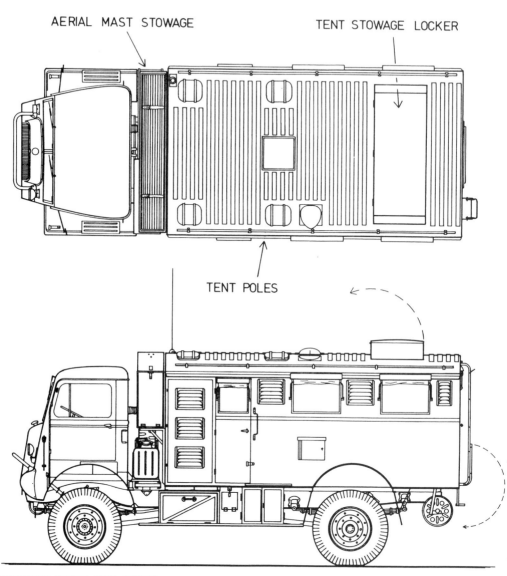

AERIAL MAST STOWAGE

TENT STOWAGE LOCKER

TENT POLES

TRUCK PLAN NO. B6

BEDFORD QLR 3-ton

NOTE: Drawing shows typical House-type body layout. Positions of some minor details could vary according to exact use of vehicle. Aerial Mast racks were fitted on both sides on some vehicles.

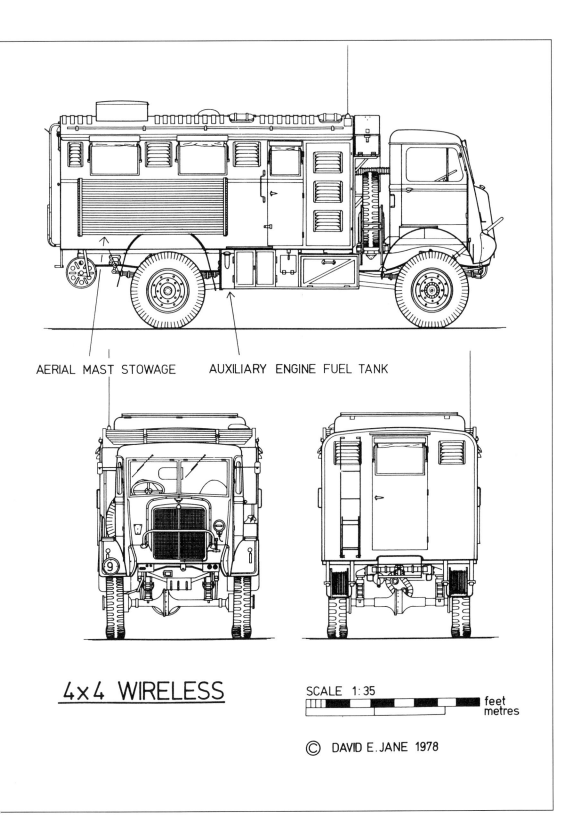

AERIAL MAST STOWAGE   AUXILIARY ENGINE FUEL TANK

4×4 WIRELESS

SCALE 1:35

feet
metres

Ⓒ DAVID E. JANE 1978

BEDFORD QL
IN CLOSE-UP

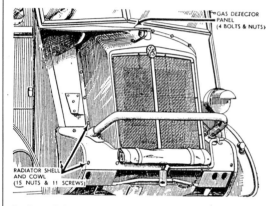

Radiator fittings.

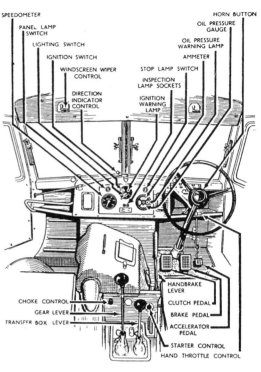

Instrument panel and controls.

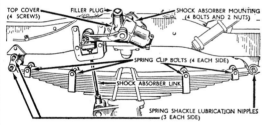

Front spring and shock absorber.

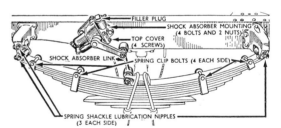

Rear spring and shock absorber.

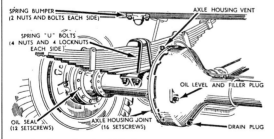

Front axle and spring U-bolts.

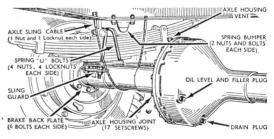

Rear axle and spring U-bolts.